HOTEL/MOTEL OPERATIONS
AN OVERVIEW

2ND EDITION

Suzanne Stewart Weissinger, MTA

Africa • Australia • Canada • Denmark • Japan • Mexico • New Zealand • Philippines
Puerto Rico • Singapore • Spain • United Kingdom • United States

Delmar Staff:
Business Unit Director: Susan L. Simpfenderfer
Executive Editor: Marlene McHugh Pratt
Acquisitions Editor: Erin O'Connor Traylor
Developmental Editor: Judy Roberts
Executive Production Manager: Wendy A. Troeger
Production Editor: Elaine Scull
Executive Marketing Manager: Donna Lewis
Channel Managers: Nigar Hale, Eleanor J. Murray
Cover Design: Elaine Scull

Library of Congress Cataloging-in-Publication Data
Weissinger, Suzanne Stewart.
  Hotel/motel operations: an overview/Suzanne Stewart Weissinger.—2nd ed.
    p. cm.
  Includes bibliographical references.
  ISBN 0-7668-1214-6
  1. Hotel management.   2. Motel management.   I. Title.
  TX911.3.M27 W43 1999
  647.94'068—dc21

                                                                99-048379

Delmar Publishers is pleased to offer the following books on

HOSPITALITY, TRAVEL, AND TOURISM

NEW AND REVISED TITLES IN 2000!

- **Best Impressions in Hospitality (2000)**
  Angie Michael
  ISBN 0-7668-1584-6

- **Catering & Convention Services (1999)**
  Ahmed Ismail
  ISBN 0-7668-0037-7

- **Cruising: A Guide to the Cruise Line Industry (2000)**
  Marc Mancini
  ISBN 0-7668-0971-4

- **Managing the Guest Experience (2000)**
  Robert Ford and
  Cherrill Heaton
  ISBN 0-7668-1415-7

- **Hotel/Motel Operations: An Overview, 2E (2000)**
  Suzanne Weissinger
  ISBN 0-7668-1214-6

- **Human Resources Management for the Hospitality Industry, 2E (2000)**
  Mary Tanke
  ISBN 0-8273-7321-X

- **Marketing & Selling the Travel Product, 2E (2000)**
  James Burke and Barry Resnick
  ISBN 0-8273-7648-0

- **Selling Destinations: Geography for the Travel Professional, 3E (1999)**
  Marc Mancini
  ISBN 0-7668-0848-3

- **Selling Tourism (2000)**
  H. Kenner Kay
  ISBN 0-8273-8648-6

- **Welcome to Hospitality: An Introduction, 2E (2000)**
  Kye-Sung (Kaye) Chon and Ray Sparrowe
  ISBN 0-7668-0850-5

Additional titles available:

- **Conducting Tours, 2E (1996)**
  Marc Mancini
  ISBN 0-8273-7471-2

- **Dining Room and Banquet Management, 2E (1997)**
  Anthony Strianese
  ISBN 0-8273-7566-2

- **Geography of Travel & Tourism, 3E (1999)**
  Lloyd Hudman and Richard Jackson
  ISBN 0-7668-0371-6

- **Hospitality and Travel Marketing, 2E (1996)**
  Alastair Morrison
  ISBN 0-8273-6620-5

- **Hotel, Restaurant and Travel Law, 5E (1999)**
  Norman Cournoyer, Anthony Marshall and Karen Morris
  ISBN 0-8273-7536-0

- **Hotel Sales & Operations (1999)**
  Ahmed Ismail ISBN 0-8273-8647-8

- **Travel Perspectives: A Guide to Becoming a Travel Agent, 2E (1996)**
  Susan Rice and Ginger Todd
  ISBN 0-8273-6533-0

- **International Air Fares: Construction and Ticketing (1995)**
  Helle Sorensen
  ISBN 0-538-71081-0

- **International Travel and Tourism (1997)**
  Helle Sorensen
  ISBN 0-8273-7448-8

- **Practical Food & Beverage Cost Control (1999)**
  Clement Ojugo
  ISBN 0-7668-0038-5

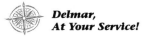

Delmar,
At Your Service!

To Place an Order Call
1-800-354-9706
for 4-Year Colleges/Universities
or
1-800-347-7707
for 2-Year and Career Colleges
www.delmar.com

CONTENTS

PREFACE

As in the past, service industries make up the largest segment of the world economy. Tourism is one of the largest service components, and in the forefront is the lodging industry. Enjoying phenomenal growth, the hotel/motel industry produces a great demand for trained, knowledgeable employees.

Lodging establishments offer a large variety of positions and opportunity. This hotel/motel text presents a total overview, not just one finite view, but all departments within a property. Such information is valuable to people pursuing careers in any facet of the tourism industry, as understanding the relationship between the various components is essential.

This 2nd edition is heavily revised. Extensive additions reflect the technological advancements that have taken place in all aspects, including all operations of properties. To mirror our shrinking world, international practices, procedures and viewpoints are incorporated throughout the text. Career opportunities are discussed for each department. New material includes a by-chapter review of *Trends,* both apparent and expected. The addition of Chapter Projects, chapter outlines, increased Glossary definitions, and objectives make the 2nd edition quite new. An Instructor's Guide offers comprehensive tests, teaching tips, and suggested activities.

- Since knowledge of history leads to a better understanding of the present, Chapter 1, "Lodgings, Yesterday and Today," studies the hotel industry's past.
- Because people are the heart of the hospitality industry, Chapter 2, "The Hospitality Business and You," looks at prerequisites, both skills and personality, that are needed for successful careers in the business. More specific service training and welcoming international visitors have been added.
- "Classification of Lodging Facilities," Chapter 3, explains the terminology used in labeling properties. Material now includes discussions of the growth of extended-stay properties, special interest facilities and corporate "branding."
- Chapters 4-6 trace the activities involved from guest reservations, to registration, to accounting. Computer usage has changed these scenarios dramatically in past years. Yield Management, with all its nuances, is now explained.
- Chapter 7, is expanded to include security, thus is now "Housekeeping, Engineering, and Security."

- "Food and Beverage Department," Chapter 8, exhibits alternative employment opportunities. Chapter 9, is now "Sales and Meeting Planning" to update and broaden the ever growing meeting and conference business. "Accommodations: References and Ratings," Chapter 10, now includes extensive instructions on internet bookings.

Upon completion of this text, students will have a clear view of the vibrant hotel/motel business and its relationship to other segments of the tourism industry. New doors of opportunity will open up for them and give them confidence to identify positions that fit their interests, needs, skills, and personality.

Check out the dynamic lodging industry and the options it offers to *check in* to an exciting career.

Suzanne Steward Weissinger

ACKNOWLEDGMENTS

The author would like to thank the following reviewers for their valuable feedback and constructive criticism:

Steve Bergonzoni
Burlington Community College
Pemberton, NJ

Rob Turner
Delhi State University
Delhi, NY

1

LODGINGS:
YESTERDAY AND TODAY

LEARNING OBJECTIVES

After reading this chapter, you should be able to

- Discuss the history of the lodging industry from ancient to modern times.
- Describe the post roads and the taverns where George Washington slept in his travels along the eastern coast of the United States.
- Cite the names of several famous people who influenced the hotel industry.
- Discuss how the introduction of railroads, automobiles, and air travel affected the lodging industry.
- Describe governmental influence on the lodging industry in the United States and other countries.
- Understand the future trends of the industry.

"GEORGE WASHINGTON SLEPT HERE!"

So read the signs that hang above so many rooms, people wonder if George ever slept at his beloved Mt. Vernon at all! The inns where George Washington slept were scattered across the eastern United States in small coastal cities and towns along the post roads. These inns were called taverns, with public rooms on the first floor and sleeping rooms above.

The heat from the open fireplace, the odors of the cooking meat, the smoke, the wet leather, and the tobacco would engulf an arriving guest. The long planked wooden tables were all crowded, not only with guests staying for the night, but also with local people stopping by for a tankard of beer and a smoke. After a few puffs the men would pass the long-stemmed clay pipe to a compatriot who would break off the used end and have his smoke. The boisterous voices of the guests competed with the bellowing of the mistress of the inn telling a servant to stoke the already blazing fire or to serve a guest.

The privy house was a scant 20 feet from the tavern. Upstairs were two rooms each with four beds. Each bed slept at least three people crosswise. Wooden hooks protruded from the walls for the guests to hang clothes, though they slept with all but outer clothes on. No candle would be sent up to the sleeping rooms, and after dark, the tavern visitors would make do with the light of the open fire. Surely, Washington would have been offered a room in the family's private quarters.

ANCIENT HISTORY

CLASSIC GREEK AND ROMAN DAYS

Think of all the hospitality that you and I enjoyed from strangers before we reached our homes. . . .

Though a myth, the travels of Odysseus, as recorded by Homer in the *Odyssey* and the *Iliad* give insights into lodgings of those ancient days. While roaming the Mediterranean his statement above shows his appreciation of hospitable welcomes where he stayed.

In ancient Rome the inns were large mansions. Owners of these inns would not allow guests to stay unless they carried a "letter of eviction," which was permission to travel from government officials. Similar inns existed along the famous Appian Way, and as with the larger inns, the owners were often investigators for the government.

The Romans, mostly legionnaires and civil officials, built monuments to their civilization throughout Britain and Europe in their exploration and conquering expeditions. Most were built in beautiful areas with natural springs. Their taverns were called "tabernas," and the attached inn was called a "cauponas." In Bath, England, relics dating from A.D. 54 still exist today.

In early days in the Near East, caravans crossing vast deserts, stopped at *caravansaries.* These were accommodations that surrounded large courtyards.

BIBLE REFERENCES

And she brought forth her first-born son, and wrapped him in swaddling clothes and laid him in a manger; because there was no room for them in the inn. (Luke 2:7.)

Certainly the most famous inn is the one in Bethlehem. The great crowds reporting there to pay their taxes had overburdened the lodging industry of that small town. This is not the only mention of the hotel industry in the Bible. In the Old Testament we are told about Jacob and his brother traveling in Judea, going to an inn, and foddering their mounts. To these inns, travelers would bring their own supplies. They are similar to khans, or rest houses, found in the Middle East today.

FIGURE 1-1

The Tabard Inn, featured in Chaucer's *Canterbury Tales,* was a fine hostelry of the 1300s in London.

MIDDLE AGES

In Southwark at that high-class hostelry known as the Tabard, close beside The Bell . . . .

The famous storyteller Chaucer in his *Canterbury Tales* speaks of the Tabard, a fine hostelry of the 1300s in London. As Chaucer relates, the host of the Tabard decided to accompany the pilgrims on their journey and listen to their stories. During the book, Chaucer tells of eating *table d'hote* (a menu from which one may order a complete meal at a set price) and settling their "reckoning" (hotel bill). The Savoy Hotel in London has foundations believed to date from Chaucer's time. Fourteenth-century innkeeping, as Chaucer describes it, sounds as sophisticated in many ways as it is today.

The term *hostelers,* meaning "inn holders," was not used until 1473. The term may have come from the Old French word *ostel.* Gradually "hostelers" shifted in meaning from "owner" of the inn to "inn-servant." The *h* is sometimes dropped to "ostler." The term *hostel,* meaning "inn," was not used until the 1800s. In modern usage hostels are accommodations of lesser quality, and hostelers are guests who stay at hostels.

During the Crusades the hotel industry grew. The design was fairly standard: The enclosed courtyard was surrounded by the kitchen, tav-

Punch

FIGURE 1-2

On their journey, Chaucer's pilgrims ate "table d'hote," which means they ordered from a limited menu.

ern, and public rooms on the front facade. On each side, winging out from the front, were the sleeping rooms. Along the back of the building were the stables. Could this not be the forerunner of motels?— Park your horses and stay a night.

COLONIAL PERIOD

Public coach service was put into effect around 1650. The coaches ran between major cities and stopped wherever passengers wanted, similar to the way our bus lines operate today. Coach inns were built along the routes primarily at points where teams of horses were changed. The British use the term *ordinary* to describe such inns.

The United States Postal Service, established in 1710, called its primary routes between major towns along the Atlantic Coast *post roads.* With the establishment of these post roads, entrepreneurial farmers converted their farm houses into inns. Passengers from the coaches slept in the hostel's *long room* with their feet toward the fire. The vignette "George Washington Slept Here," in the opening paragraphs of this chapter, describes the inns and hostels of this era.

NINETEENTH CENTURY

The introduction of railroads had great influence on the hotel/motel industry. In the early 1800s, as train tracks were laid throughout the Western world, depot hotels began to arise. In most cases (as with the Euston Station in London, built in 1830) the hotel was connected directly to the train station. Similarly, think of the masses of hotels around airports today with shuttle buses carrying passengers directly to their lodgings. As early as the 1800s the transportation and lodgings industries could not be separated.

As Canadians laid train tracks across the vast North American continent, they built magnificent hotels and resorts near the route. Le Chateau Frontenac in Quebec, Chateau Laurier in Ottawa, and Chateau Lake Louise in Alberta are examples.

SPAS AND RESORTS

Spas, which are mineral springs or pools believed to be medicinal or healthful, have been tourist sites since Roman days. Throughout the world the advent of trains caused beautiful resorts to be built at these sites. In 1830 Pennsylvania boasted that it was the first state to have railway travel to its spas. However, the most famous spa in those days was Saratoga Springs, New York. Advertised, and quite popular, were Saratoga trunks that would accommodate all the clothes one needed to spend a "season" at a resort.

Spas at Baden, Germany; Marienbad, Bohemia; and Vichy, France, which had been popular for centuries, became more accessible to the public via rail. Resort areas such as the French Riviera became *the* places to go. Niagara Falls; the Greenbriar at White Sulfur Springs, West Virginia; the Homestead in Hot Springs, Virginia; and The Cloister at Sea Island, Georgia, are legendary resorts that still exist today. Since the early 1900s, the Poconos and Catskills, Aspen and Vail, and hundreds of other noted resort areas have sprung up.

FIGURE 1-3

A popular vacation in the early 1800s was a visit to a spa. To prepare for these trips, immense Saratoga trunks were stuffed with everything "m'lady" could possibly need for a season there.

In 1841, Englishman Thomas Cook arranged his first tour. Though it was a one-day train excursion, shortly thereafter he organized overnight trips, booking multiple rooms at hotels for his clients. Considered the first travel agent, by 1856 he was taking groups of North Americans to hotels on his "Cook's Tour of Europe."

LUXURY HOTELS

Another benchmark for the hotel industry in the nineteenth century was the opening of the Tremont Hotel in Boston. It was the first luxury hotel and boasted the first indoor toilets and the first private bedrooms with locks on the doors. The Tremont also had a version of today's bellhop, then called a "rotunda man."

In 1889 the famous Swiss hotelier Cesar Ritz became manager at the Savoy in London. Eventually, he opened his own London Ritz and subsequently opened famed luxury hotels in Paris, New York, and other cities.

THE TWENTIETH CENTURY

A bed with a bath for a dollar and a half.

This was the motto that led the hotel industry into the twentieth century. E.M. Statler opened his first hotel in Buffalo, New York, in 1907. Individual rooms with private baths and Statler's ability to cater to business travelers set this hotel apart. Statler's name is legendary in the industry today.

OTHER NOTEWORTHY INNKEEPERS

Conrad Hilton, "King of the Innkeepers," also influenced this era. Hilton, who had helped his family run a hotel in New Mexico, opened his first hotel, the Mobley, in Texas in 1919. From there the Dallas Hilton opened in 1925. Today the familiar Hilton name is seen in almost every major city. In 1954, Hilton bought the Statler chain. Statler-Hiltons are located in New York, Dallas, Washington, and other cities.

Several other names also are legendary in the industry, among them Howard Johnson, J. Williard Marriott, and Kemmons Wilson, founder of Holiday Inns. Each founder has a unique success story, and

FIGURE 1-4

Conrad Hilton started his world renowned chain of hotels when he bought the Mobley in Texas in 1919.

each chain has its own standards of hospitality that it has established over the years.

TOURIST COURTS

The automobile led the hotel industry into a booming business in the 1920s. The term *motel,* coined from "motor hotel," goes back to the time when a farmer owning land along the major routes would build wooden 10 foot by 10 foot cabins along the road in front of his property. A car could be pulled right up to the cabin, where a traveler could spend the evening. The owners of these motels soon expanded to, perhaps, 15 cabins. These were called *tourist courts.* These businesses proved profitable during the free economy of the 1920s. Compare tourist courts with the huge motor inns that border the interstate highways of today.

THE GREAT DEPRESSION AND WORLD WAR II

The 1930s saw the Great Depression and a setback for the lodging industry. Many smaller motels went bankrupt. The industry did not recover until the war years.

During World War II, thousands of people, both military and civilian, traveled throughout the United States. There were troops being transported, workers going to various war factories, and families

FIGURE 1-5

With the advent of air travel, business travelers became the most important lodging guests.

reuniting. New hotels were built near all major military bases and industrial areas.

ADVENT OF AIR TRAVEL

At the end of the war a new mode of transportation had matured. Air travel was now available to the masses, and business was booming, while conventions and conferences became an integral part of successful commerce. Companies opened regional and branch offices. Thus business travelers, in their vast numbers, became the most important lodging guests.

Also, because people had more disposable income following the war, they were able to travel more for pleasure. The advent of air travel prompted resort hotels to spring up around the world. Southern Spain, Yugoslavia, the Canary Islands, Hawaii, and Las Vegas, to mention a few, all offered lavish resort complexes.

Many resorts offered *package plans,* some in conjunction with the airlines, where one price pays for airfare and accommodations. Club Med established many resort properties. At Club Med resorts, guests pay a set fee which covers all expenses including air, hotel, all meals, bar bill, cigarettes, and golf or tennis fees. The convenience and comfort of knowing exactly what your expenses will be ahead of time, and having them paid in advance, are prominent features of a package plan. These plans are still popular among vacation travelers today.

THE INDUSTRY TODAY

Nothing has daunted the growth spiral of the hotel/motel business. The industry today is diverse and offers lodgings to satisfy just about any type of traveler.

ALTERNATIVE LODGING

Since some travelers seek accommodations different from the traditional hotel/motel room, the lodging industry today offers alternatives, such as campgrounds and bed and breakfast (B & B) opportunities, to accommodate all tastes. Campgrounds appeal to travelers who prefer to commune with nature while on vacation. Campgrounds, both commercial and in national and state parks, are a small but thriving part of the lodging industry.

In the Middle East, renovated harems that once accommodated a man's 60 wives, now serve as hotels. In Africa, a hotel called "Treetops" features rooms in a huge tree from which guests can watch wild animals feed at night. In Japan, there are ryokans which exhibit typical, simple Japanese decor, and inexpensive lodgings with four to six built-in bunk beds. And there are *boatels,* or accommodations on boats. The most famous of these is the Queen Mary, which is docked at Long Beach, California, and can accommodate conventions and conferences. A person can pay for a room in a wigwam, a lighthouse, or even sleep on a Chattanooga Choo-Choo Pullman car where the beautiful train depot there serves as the lobby.

There are B & Bs and pensiones, all offering breakfast and often a shared bath down the hall. Student fraternity houses also are turned into hostels for the summer and registered as hotels. Elderhostel is an organization that specializes in educational tours for senior citizens. They stay in college and university dormitories while studying an area

or a particular topic. No matter the preference, be it luxury, unusual, or everyday, travelers will usually find a hotel to their liking.

GOVERNMENT INFLUENCE

A nation's government can influence, regulate, or control its accommodations industry. For example, governments apply and enforce sanitation and safety rules. They establish reimbursement rates for government employee travel. Some nations own lodging establishments. Spain owns *paradores* and Portugal owns *pousadas.* These are hotels usually in renovated historic properties. The theory behind the government ownership was to provide affordable accommodations for the populace. This is similar to government's involvement in national parks. Some countries rate and rank their hotels. Large incentives in the way of tax privileges are sometimes given to hotel owners. In the Caribbean, sometimes import duties are forgiven for construction materials used for building a property. Scarce items, such as limited beef produced on a small island, may have minimal import tax because a government appreciates the importance of both satisfying tourists and generating income for its economy.

In the United States we see government influence in the hotel/motel industry with highway appropriations and tax write-offs for business travel expenses. Overall, in the free world the hotel/motel industry is a free enterprise. It can be a massive conglomerate or a small "Ma and Pa" operation.

GROWTH OF THE INDUSTRY

Over 50 percent of the United States economy in this decade is devoted to service-oriented business, up from 33 percent in 1950. So the phenomenal growth of the lodgings industry, a major player within the service industry, is not surprising. Today there are more than 45,000 hotels, motels, motor lodges, and resorts in the United States alone. These account for 2 million rooms available for rent on any one given night. By 2000 it is estimated that in the United States the accommodations industry will employ over 205 million people.

The international business boom, economic prosperity, and a desire for broadening cultural and social knowledge promise great growth for the tourism industry in the future. Obviously, the lodgings industry will keep pace. More and more hotels will be built, and more and more trained personnel will be employed.

TRENDS

The past few years have seen changes in the hospitality industry. On the one hand, mega-mergers between familiar "brand name" hotels are spawning large hotel companies. At the same time independently owned properties are disappearing, though there has been a tremendous growth of small, intimate bed and breakfast establishments. New hotels are being opened in the suburbs and at airports as opposed to downtown districts.

As with everything today, electronic communications are not a luxury but a necessity. Even a vacationer is likely to carry a computer, so electronic access must be provided in guest rooms. Computerized automatic check-out, room service ordering, and voice-mail are becoming standard throughout hotels.

One of the fastest growing segments of the industry is extended-stay hotels. These cater to business people on the move, with kitchenettes and sitting rooms providing comforts for month-long stays.

CHAPTER ACTIVITIES

1. List all the terms that mean "lodging establishment" in this chapter.

2. In this time line, describe the accommodations used by travelers. Also add significant inventions or social trends that affected lodgings of the time. Speculate on what accommodations will be like in the year 2020.

Ancient History	B.C. 100	_____
		_____
		_____
Crusades	A.D. 1100	_____
		_____
Middle Ages	1300	_____
		_____
		_____
Renaissance	1400	_____
		_____
		_____
Colonial Period	1650	_____
	1790	_____
Nineteenth Century	1800	_____
	1880	_____
Twentieth Century	1900	_____
	Present	_____
The future	2020	_____

CHAPTER PROJECTS

LODGINGS: YESTERDAY AND TODAY

1. Using your imagination, describe the typical hotel in the year 2025.

2. List the major hotel/motels in your area. Trace the origin of one of them, and decide what events in the history of hotels affected it.

3. List the resorts located closest to the area in which you live. What are the amenities (golf, tennis, etc.) offered?

4. Obtain from a travel agency two or three package plans that include hotel accommodations. Compare how the quality of the hotel affects the price.

2

THE HOSPITALITY BUSINESS AND YOU

CHAPTER OUTLINE

LEARNING OBJECTIVES

After reading this chapter, you should be able to

- Describe the basic requirements for a successful hotel/motel.
- Evaluate yourself as a hotel/motel employee.
- Define and describe the term *service* as it applies to hotel/motel.
- Trace all areas of selling in a hotel/motel setting.
- Handle complaints successfully.
- Deal with international visitors graciously.

A HOME AWAY FROM HOME

What makes a hotel/motel successful? The answer is simple: A successful hotel or motel must be a "home away from home" for its clients.

Some travelers may not like their own homes, so a hotel might offer them a style of living they only dream of. This does not mean that a hotel must be "homey" or "homelike," but it does have to provide the basics that most people are accustomed to finding in their own homes.

What are your basic requirements for your home? Most people want their homes to be attractive, clean, relatively quiet and safe. We discuss these four requirements in the following sections.

ATTRACTIVE DECOR

In choosing a decor, a hotel must decide upon the image it wants to convey to its guests. A chain of hotels might have 10 individual properties all with the same decor, thereby establishing continuity of its image. This sameness appeals greatly to many people who travel frequently. They will generally know what to expect from a particular hotel or motel from a visual standpoint.

Everyone's idea of the perfect ambience differs greatly. Some like space-age architecture with skylights, bubble domes, 20-foot free-form plastic chandeliers, and bold orange and red upholstered furniture. Others prefer a more subdued decor with marble-topped sideboards, delicate Louis XVI chairs, and muted mauves and blues.

No matter the decor, tastefulness, eye-appeal, neatness, and well-kept fixtures all make for an attractive appearance. To please their guests, hotels and motels should strive for these qualities in their facilities.

CLEANLINESS

Most people try to keep their own homes clean. When they are paying for a hotel room, they expect cleanliness. Public rooms in hotels should also be kept spotless. Cleanliness goes beyond merely scrubbing the toilet and providing crisp sheets. Ashtrays in the lobby must be kept emptied, hallways vacuumed, and mirrors and brass polished. Room-service trays must not be left for hours outside of guest rooms.

FIGURE 2-1

A hotel's image is based upon the decor it chooses as well as the cleanliness of its facilities.

QUIET

During some years, the Sheraton in Philadelphia rents almost its entire hotel to hundreds of midshipmen from the Annapolis Naval Academy and cadets from West Point when the Army-Navy game is played. These students do not expect, nor do they find, quiet surroundings. This example of high-spirited hotel guests is more the exception than the rule, however.

Hotel guests, in most cases, expect a reasonably quiet atmosphere. Most vacation travelers want to relax. Business travelers often try to concentrate and work in their rooms. Noise and activity are disruptive and conducive neither to relaxing nor working.

SAFETY REQUIREMENTS

In addition to "home away from home" stipulations made by travelers, certain safety and security requirements are imposed by the government to protect hotel and motel guests. In-room sprinkler systems, clearly marked exits, fireproof stairs, or fire escapes are but a few of the state or federal government standards that must be met. Measures to protect the personal security of guests may be enforced. Parking-garage lighting may be regulated. Room-key security is discussed in Chapter 5, "Front-Office Operations."

Measures to protect guests' personal property are often mandated by local laws. Hotels usually have a disclaimer on their registration card declaring they are not responsible for valuables and stating the availability of safe-deposit boxes. Chapter 7, "Housekeeping, Engineering, and Security" covers this.

The Americans with Disabilities Act (ADA) requires accessibility, such as ramps and elevators, in most public buildings. Rooms for the disabled are designed with wide doorways, floor-level showers, and lower sink vanities. Elevators with Braille buttons are provided for guests who are sight impaired. Strobe lights assist those who are hearing impaired.

Some states require that a percentage of the guest rooms be smoke-free. Multistoried properties may have entire smoke-free floors.

PERSONNEL—THE KEY TO SERVICE

The word *service* can be defined as conduct that is useful or helpful to others. In the hospitality industry, however, service is much more. Service is the prime business. If an establishment is providing lodging or food to a guest, it is providing a service. The hotel/motel and food industries are certainly considered "service industries" and are a significant part of the economy.

Who performs the service? People. To be successful, people in all phases of the hotel/motel business must be courteous and friendly, efficient and prompt, attractively attired and neat, able to serve others, and able to sell. These attributes are discussed in detail in the following sections.

COURTESY AND FRIENDLINESS

A bright smile with a cheerful "good afternoon" goes far in establishing the image of a hotel. Certainly "thank you," "I'm sorry," and

FIGURE 2-2

To be a successful hotel employee, you must be courteous and friendly, efficient and prompt, neatly attired, able to serve others, and able to sell.

"please" cannot be said enough in the hospitality industry. Gone are the days of snooty doormen and desk clerks.

People working in the hotel/motel business must be outgoing and not afraid to speak with total strangers. Their voices must be clear and understandable, and they must convey sincerity.

Everyone loves to hear their name. A name belongs to a person. In any one-on-one situation, using another's name extends friendliness, understanding, and empathy with that person. In the hotel business, many employees are in a position to know a guest's name. A name is given to check-in at the front desk. The switchboard operator knows guests' names. A name is known when room service is delivered. Once an employee hears a name, it should be noted and used frequently thereafter. Hotel employees should always use the titles Mr. and Ms., then the last names. Most properties use name tags for employees so that guests know employees' names. An excellent host/guest relationship can develop through the simple use of names.

Courtesy and friendliness should also be extended through the telephone. A voice alone can reflect a smile and enthusiasm. Over

the phone, once again, a friendly greeting, generous use of words of etiquette, and the frequent use of names form a hospitable atmosphere for a property.

EFFICIENCY AND PROMPTNESS

Nobody likes to wait. Causing a guest to stand before the front desk while the desk clerk fumbles through papers has never helped a hotel's image. Ordering breakfast from room service at 7 A.M. and still waiting for it at 8 A.M. does not impress a guest with a hotel's efficiency.

What causes these inefficiencies? Often they are the fault of some person within the hotel complex. They also may be caused by a poor system or, in some cases, a computer failure. Whatever the causes of inefficiency, good management and personnel choices go a long way in ensuring efficiency and promptness in a hotel/motel.

Hotel employees should excel in attending to details. They should have a sense of organizing and prioritizing the tasks to be done. Completing activities and a subsequent double-check or follow-up is mandatory for successful hotel employees.

ATTRACTIVE AND NEAT APPEARANCE

Not all are created equally attractive, but all can do their best to be neat. No gum or food when in public, tasteful make-up, good haircuts, and abiding by the management's dress code all contribute to an attractive image for employees. Cleanliness, of course, goes without saying.

Many departments in a hotel require employees to wear uniforms. Housekeeping and engineering personnel usually wear uniforms. Doormen and parking attendants wear uniforms ranging in style from elaborate costumes to matching slacks and open-collared shirts. Front-desk clerks often are in matching blazers and shirts. Many hotel employees enjoy wearing a proscribed uniform and not having to assemble an extensive work wardrobe.

ABILITY TO SERVE OTHERS

Subservience is probably the most difficult attitude for people to assume. In the hotel industry a desk clerk learns not to cringe when a guest barks, "Hand me my room key," or the front desk manager commands, "Go up to the fourth floor and see if Room 428 has been

Canada	15,127	1
West Europe	10,007	2
Mexico	8,433	3
Asia	7,756	4
South America	2,831	5
Caribbean	1,189	6
Oceania	680	7
Central America	564	8
Middle East	552	9
East Europe	382	10
Africa	104	11

FIGURE 2-3

Where do our visitors come from? (numbers of arrivals in thousands)
Source: Tourism Industries, International Trade Administration, Commerce Department.

cleaned." A person in the hospitality business is there to serve others. Good training and supervision both go a long way toward making this requirement less difficult.

DEALING WITH INTERNATIONAL VISITORS

Borders between countries seem to be disappearing, and we truly live in a global economic and social environment. Businesses establish branch offices throughout the world, sending business travelers on weekly jaunts across the oceans. On the leisure travel side, North America has become a prime destination for people from all countries. From senior citizens to backpacking teenagers, people from all cultures visit around the world.

To hotel employees, many international visitors will be almost invisible. They dress the same as we do, speak English beautifully, and have similar mannerisms. Others will appear exotic in strange robes, and conversations will be in broken English and sign language. For this reason, hospitality workers should speak clearly and slowly. Many people from other countries are more conservative in their actions. Hospitality workers should act accordingly and not stare or whisper when in a guest's presence.

In the hospitality industry, knowledge of a foreign language is a valuable asset. Even a few words of greeting in Spanish to a Spanish-speaking guest extends untold hospitality and goodwill. Many hotels form a language-bank where employees with language skills are listed

and are called upon to help international visitors. A gardener may be called by the front desk to help a Middle-Easterner check in.

In larger city properties that international visitors frequent, cashiers should know the policy on accepting foreign currency, bank drafts, and credit cards. They should know where the closest bank that will exchange foreign currency is located.

Often, the hospitality industry provides an opportunity to become a part of the "international scene." To meet people from other cultures, to broaden a narrow outlook, to learn about our ever shrinking world is a fascinating bonus in many hotels.

HANDLING COMPLAINTS

In all businesses that involve one-on-one servicing of individuals, complaints will evolve. Patrons of lodging establishments have paid for pleasant decor, cleanliness, nice surroundings, and efficient, positive personnel contacts. So, when problems occur, as they will, hotel customers voice discontent. Common complaints are listed below in no particular order:

- Lack of cleanliness
- Physical condition of room (i.e., about low water pressure, air conditioning/heat controls, television switches)
- Discourteous, uninformed employees
- Telephone service, such as incorrect wake-up times or surcharges
- Departmental problems, such as slow room service
- Billing discrepancies

People have different expectations and different tolerance levels. Hospitality employees can learn certain steps to take when the inevitable complaints arise. These can turn a complainer into a loyal customer.

1. Listen attentively to the problem. Ask questions to get the facts so that you thoroughly understand the situation. Remain objective, and don't take the guest's complaint and/or attitude as being personally involved with you.
2. Assume that the guest is right. Don't argue. Use statements such as "I understand." Express concern. Repeat the problem, as you understand it, to the guest.
3. Offer solution options. If the problem has to do with hotel policy (such as room service closing at midnight), calmly explain the policy.

4. If possible, solve the problem immediately in the presence of the guest. For example, call housekeeping to get adequate towels.

If in a public space and the complainer is loud, move the guest to a office or private space. If the complainer is abusive, call a supervisor immediately. A witnessing employee should also be present at this type of conflict confrontation.

As part of providing good service, many hotels empower their employees to solve problems and find solutions for complaints. Quick reconciliation of complaints can produce loyal repeat visitors.

SELLING SKILLS

Another highly desirable attribute for almost all lodging industry workers is the ability to sell. Most lodging facilities have a sales/catering office which sells meeting space for conventions and banquets, but this function is quite different from the selling which occurs in almost all departments.

All employees must sell on a day-to-day basis to each guest or potential guest. This one-on-one selling entails selling the different services of the hotel. Employees must also participate in the hotel's return business selling effort. One-on-one and return business selling are discussed in the following two sections.

One-On-One Selling.   When guests enter a hotel, they are usually greeted first by the doorman. The doorman sells the image of the hotel by being friendly and helpful. From there the guest goes to the front desk and may or may not have a reservation. If there is no prior reservation, the front-desk clerk tries to convince the person to buy this hotel's services. The guest may have a reservation but no room assignment. Here the clerk can "sell up." For instance, a double room might be sold to a single vacationer because it has a better view. A suite near the pool might be sold to a family with children instead of a double with a cot.

After guests have checked in, the bellhop takes them to their room. Selling is done on the elevator through polite conversation. For instance, discussing tonight's menu might persuade the guest to eat at the hotel. By discussing the gym privileges available at a small fee, a sale might be made. Each sale, no matter how big or small, is profit for the hotel since the basis of budgeting for the operation is room rental.

Return Business Selling.   The entire operation of the hotel depends on the ability of employees to sell the guest on returning. One way a

hotel can make guests want to return is through providing special amenities. Making people feel special will often ensure their return. Many hotels have a good filing system whereby the guest's likes, dislikes, and habits are noted and recorded. Courtesy cars, transfers to and from the airport, express check-in or checkout, flowers, wine in the room, free use of the jacuzzi, and continental breakfast in the lobby all make for that special feeling. All of these are VIP treatments that can be incorporated into any hotel operation.

Other amenities that are not so elaborate but effective are babysitting services and free use of appliances such as irons and in-room coffeepots. Cable television is an incentive that is often used. Small refrigerators in the rooms or ice already in the ice bucket are "extras." Hotel employees help make guests aware that these amenities are available to entice the visitors to return.

Chapter 9 deals with selling more extensively. Selling is a skill that can be learned and can become second nature for most people.

CAREERS IN THE HOSPITALITY INDUSTRY

Entry-level hotel/motel employees unfortunately do not earn particularly high salaries. But for the person who is dedicated, outgoing, and willing to work the odd hours, promotions come easily. Salaries after the entry level generally are in the high teens and at the management level are quite good.

POSITIONS

The hospitality industry is noted for the diversity of its employees. Not only is the Equal Opportunity Employment Act adhered to, it is embraced in the business. With a great variety of guests patronizing a property, it stands to reason that people of all races, colors, creeds, and sexes would serve the travelers.

Many entry-level positions are available in hotel/motels. Some of these do not require extensive prior training. For example, most hotels with restaurants are in constant need of *bus people,* who assist the waiters and waitresses by cleaning off and resetting the tables. The career flow from busing to waiter/waitress to hostess to catering department is not uncommon. A person interested in ultimately working in the sales department might get a foot in the door by starting out as a secretary in that department.

Other entry-level positions exist in the housekeeping department as a room cleaner or a *checker,* depending on the person's education level. Room cleaners also may progress to checkers, the people who spot-check each room after it has been cleaned. From there promotions to assistant housekeeper and, ultimately, to executive housekeeper positions are possible.

Usually some knowledge of computers or at least typing ability is required of front-desk clerks and reservationists. From these beginning positions a sharp, hard-working person can progress to night auditor or perhaps to front-desk manager or reservations manager. Crossing into this management threshold opens many opportunities for climbing the career ladder.

Figure 2-4 shows the variety of positions that are available in a large hotel. The *general manager,* or GM, directs and is responsible for all departments of the property.

TRAINING

At a small roadside 20-room motel, training for a front-desk, reservationist, room cleaner, or any other position probably will consist of one eight-hour shift with a person who holds that position. In this type of situation, it is important that a trainee ask questions, and, when on their own, knows who to contact if problems occur.

On the other hand, large hotels have human resources departments that hire, fire, and train hundreds of employees each year. Training typically includes a thorough tour of the property, department head summaries of their division's duties, and reviews of company policy and employee benefits. Most likely the company's philosophy will be discussed and service instruction will be given. How to handle complaints, as discussed above, will be featured through discussion and role-playing. Then, intense, lengthy on-the-job (OTJ) training for specific positions will take place.

Large companies, such as Marriott, have elaborate management training programs, often on the corporate level, qualifying a person to work in several positions at any property location. Many of these require that a trainee have knowledge of every department of a property by working in and filling out workbook questions and diaries on each of them. Video training, with structured testing, may be used. In this situation, a person may choose their specific position to train for, and work at their own pace.

At a job interview, a pertinent question for prospective employees in the hospitality industry to ask is, "What kind of training will I receive?" This shows not anxiety, but a willingness to learn and please.

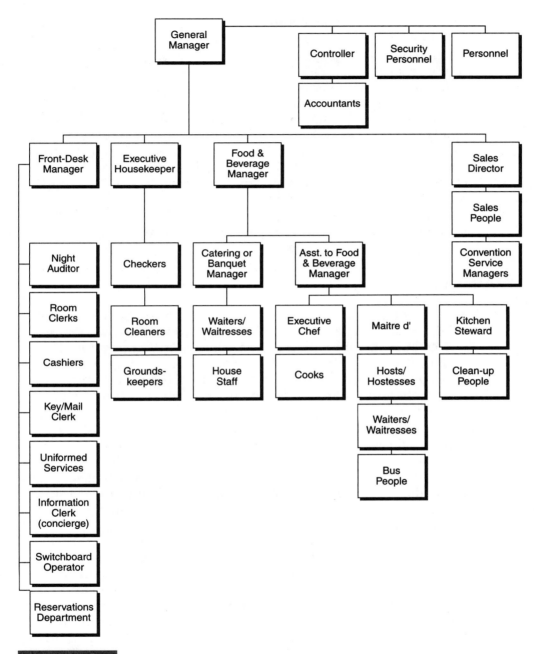

FIGURE 2-4

Organization chart for a 500-room multiservice hotel.

TRENDS

Guests, particularly business guests, are adding a fourth requirement that successful properties have to fulfill. In this electronic age, hotels are finding it almost mandatory that guest rooms be outfitted with complete telephone data ports for computer and fax machine hookup. Voice-mail accessibility is in great demand. Rooms need generous-sized desks, telephones that can be carried to various parts of the room, and adequate lighting to use when working. As more women participate in business travel, lodging establishments are catering to their specific wants and needs. Today, not only does the hotel room serve as a "home away from home" but also as an "office away from the office." In addition, staffed office centers within the hotel are becoming more common. These include office machinery, communications equipment, and personnel to perform office duties and assist the traveler.

More electronic gadgetry is also being used to expedite hotel procedures and services. Televisions can act as multimedia computer terminals, networked to all departments of the hotel. Touch-screen televisions enable guests to order from a menu, rent a video, and check out.

For hotel employees, these trends lead to the conclusion that computer efficiency will be a requirement for employees. The computers are utilized in all departments and at all levels.

CHAPTER ACTIVITIES

THE HOSPITALITY BUSINESS AND YOU

1. Take the following test by answering "yes," "no," or "sometimes" to each of the questions. Put a check mark beneath the column head which corresponds to your answer.

	Yes	No	Sometimes
a. Can I talk to strangers comfortably?	____	____	____
b. Am I pleasant and courteous even when under stress?	____	____	____
c. Am I at ease when using the telephone?	____	____	____
d. Do I generally look clean and neat?	____	____	____
e. Can I follow orders?	____	____	____
f. Do I accept criticism gracefully?	____	____	____
g. Do I like staying busy?	____	____	____
h. Do I do detailed work well?	____	____	____
i. Do I enjoy working with other people?	____	____	____
j. Do I enjoy helping people?	____	____	____

Count 2 points for each "yes," 1 point for each "sometimes," and 0 for "no." If you scored 16 or more points, you would make an excellent hospitality worker!

2. List 25 adjectives that describe successful hospitality employees. Most are found in this chapter.

CHAPTER PROJECTS

1. Contact a hotel personnel office and obtain a job application form from them. Fill it out.

2. Obtain a large city newspaper's classified advertising section. Survey the number of hotel jobs, and count and list the types of positions available in a chart.

3. Visit a hotel and investigate guest-room electronic accessibility for computer users. Note if room-service ordering, or check-out can be accomplished via the television set. Describe your findings.

4. Describe your immediate career goal and your five-year career goal.

3 CLASSIFICATION OF LODGING FACILITIES

LEARNING OBJECTIVES

After reading this chapter, you should be able to

- Explain the differences between hotels, motor inns, motels, resorts, and private lodgings.
- Classify lodgings by function and market.
- Understand how hotel/motels become affiliated with chains.
- Describe how parking facilities, size, affiliation, and clientele are used to differentiate types of lodging facilities.
- Determine by location the types of properties most likely present.

ACCOMMODATIONS

We'll be at that big hotel downtown.

We're just going to stop along the road at motels.

I'm going to that beautiful resort at the beach.

In everyday conversation few of us really classify correctly the type of lodging facility at which we will be staying. The classifications are often hazy, and what one person would call a "hotel" another might term a "motel." Though it is impossible to define categories exactly, several means of classification have been developed by the industry.

BASIC TERMINOLOGY

Facilities for lodging are generally identified by one of five names: hotels, motor inns, motels, resorts, and privately owned (guest houses).

HOTELS

Hotels are multistoried lodging facilities which range in size from 20 rooms to hundreds of rooms. They can be quite elegant with each room individually decorated, or they can be center-city "flea bags." Hotels are usually found in large cities, and often a large portion of their guests are business travelers and convention attendees. Most center-city hotels provide valet parking, and the cars are parked in a parking garage attached to the hotel or in a nearby public garage.

In a hotel, bellhops, room service, and parking lot attendants cater to guests. Most hotels offer guests the services of at least a restaurant/bar, coffee shop, and retail shop.

A hotel may or may not be a member of a chain operation. Examples of outstanding hotels are the Hyatt Regency in Atlanta, Georgia, and the Plaza Hotel in New York City.

MOTELS

Motels are the small one-story structures that are usually found on feeder highways and roads. They are seen quite frequently along lesser known beaches. A motel provides a parking space for automobiles di-

FIGURE 3-1

There are five basic names for lodging facilities: hotels, motels, motor inns, resorts, and privately owned. Under which category do you think this facility falls?

rectly outside the guest's room door. Most often motels do not have restaurants. Motels usually are individually owned, often with the owner's family providing all the services.

The Dew Drop Inn in Gatlinburg, Tennessee, is one of the more charming motels, with a bubbling brook outside each door and

fireplaces in the rooms. Along the outer banks of Cape Hatteras in North Carolina, small, reasonably priced motels can be found.

MOTOR INNS

Motor inns are the most commonly seen lodging facility in most sections of the country. Motor inns range in height from two to six stories and often have a restaurant or bar. The distinction between motor inns and hotels is becoming hazier as motor inns provide more and more services, such as bellhops and room service. Often guests park their own cars in the vicinity of their rooms.

Motor inns are most often located near major highways and the interstate highway system. Motor inns located near major airports cater to the small meeting and convention business. Usually a motor inn is part of a chain, such as Holiday Inn or Comfort Inn.

RESORTS

Resorts may look like hotels or motor inns—the difference is that resorts most often are located at beaches or near the mountains. Resorts offer their guests recreational activities such as golf, horseback riding, tennis, and skiing. They may be chain or individually owned. Resorts may be open only "in season," though with the advent of indoor pools and big-named entertainment, many "summer" resorts are open year-round.

Resorts may be specialized. Examples of these would be dude ranches, ski resorts, casino hotels, and health resorts. Outstanding examples of resorts are the Cloisters in Sea Island, Georgia; and the Greenbriar in White Sulfur Springs, West Virginia. The Caribbean Islands boast many beautiful resorts.

PRIVATELY OWNED HOUSING

Privately owned housing involves guest houses, condos, and time-shares.

It is becoming more common for people across the United States to "take in guests." *Guest houses* are privately owned homes where the owners rent individual bedrooms to visitors. Usually baths are shared with other guests or with the family. This is a re-creation of the boarding house of days past.

In the United Kingdom and North America, guest houses are called ***bed and breakfasts*** or ***B & Bs;*** on the European continent, they

FIGURE 3-2

Resorts are often located at beaches or near the mountains and may offer guests certain recreational activities.

are called ***pensiones.*** In Ireland there is an extensive network of B & Bs throughout the country. Many have private baths, which are described as ***en suite.*** The term is now being heard in North America. Guest houses have always been popular in Europe, and they are gaining in popularity here.

Delightful guest houses are found throughout the United States. For example, in Rehoboth Beach, Delaware, many 1920s vintage homes are available as guest houses, with each exhibiting a small discreet sign:

Condos, short for "condominiums," in the lodging industry describe living quarters that are owned by private persons and are rented out to the public during most of the year. Usually these are apartments

in high-rise buildings located at beaches or other recreational areas. Often these are considered investments since currently tax write-offs are available to owners who do not occupy their "second home" for more than two weeks per year. The owner usually contracts with a management company to handle the rental for the rest of the year. Fees are paid to cover grounds maintenance and interior public space upkeep. Well-known hospitality companies are becoming more involved with such properties.

Time-shares describe arrangements whereby a person buys a specific time period (usually one or two weeks) to spend at a vacation resort. The price of the time-share depends on the time of the year chosen. For example, in Cancun, Mexico, where there are several beautiful time-share properties, purchasing two weeks in February, which is high season, is much more expensive than two weeks in August. It is possible to swap among time-shares. In theory, one could own a November two-week time-share in Myrtle Beach, South Carolina, but spend two weeks one year in Southern Spain, and the next in Tucson, Arizona. There are time-share consortiums that publish directories, organized by geographical location, that picture and describe properties available for swaps. Several industry giants, such as Marriott, now own time-share properties.

Home rentals are another similar option and must be considered in any study of the lodging industry. Companies, such as Barclays International Group and Creative Leisure, provide directories and reservation capabilities for private homes throughout the world.

LOCATION FACTORS

Another means of classifying lodgings is by their location. A property, no matter the terminology used to name it (see the last section), can be located in center-city, suburbs, airports, resort areas, or on highways. This means of classification describes itself.

CENTER CITY

Center-city properties are usually located in business districts. They usually cater to business travelers and are capable of hosting large conferences. Due to expensive real estate prices, they are most likely high-rise architecture. Major names in the hospitality industry are represented in center-cities. Sheraton, Marriott, and Hilton are the names seen in world capitals such as Paris, London, Tokyo, and Washington.

SUBURBAN

More and more properties are locating in the suburbs because of real estate prices and the population migration from downtown areas. Often these are near shopping centers or recreational facilities, such as golf courses. Conference capabilities are being included in their design. Atlanta, Georgia, is noted for many suburban properties located near its well-known shopping centers, Lenox Square and Phipp's Plaza.

AIRPORT

Airport locations have increased in number as the flying public increases. These, at first, were designed to accommodate business travelers making connections during week-long trips. Later, they evolved into larger full-service, multiroomed establishments with conference space for meetings.

RESORTS

As discussed in Basic Terminology, resorts refer to properties usually seen in areas of great scenic beauty or with outstanding recreational facilities. The mountains and seashore are typical examples. Properties located in such areas can charge higher rates because of the unique location qualities.

HIGHWAY

Highway properties accommodate the vast interstate audience. Their billboards and neon signs loom over the landscape, giving automobile travelers respite on long journeys.

Properties that are located in isolated areas, where there is no competition, can charge higher rates. Examples are those located on long empty stretches of highway or in remote locales.

FUNCTION AND PRIMARY MARKET

Another means of classification is by what activity usually takes place at a property. This also involves what market, what kind of guests, and use the property. Three of these categories are primarily concerned with business travelers. These are commercial, convention,

and extended-stay establishments. On the leisure travel side, properties that feature casinos are in their own function classification. Once again, resorts are included in a third classification system, as recreation being the primary function.

COMMERCIAL

Commercial properties are generally located in center-city for the convenience of the business traveler. Airport properties can also be considered commercial properties in function, drawing overnight business travelers. Many commercial establishments have business centers, featuring office equipment for guest use, and full in-room modem connections are offered.

CONVENTION

Convention properties are commercial properties that have the capability of hosting conferences and meetings. They have multiple meeting rooms and often large spaces where trade shows can be held. Many tack on the term "and Conference Center" to the hotel name.

EXTENDED STAY

The term "extended stay" denotes lodging facilities designed for guests who need long-term accommodations. They usually include kitchen and sitting rooms in each unit, thus are also called "suite" properties. Often these are located near industrial parks or office complexes and are designed for use by people on long-term assignments to businesses, or by those in the midst of job relocation situations.

CASINO

Casino properties offer patrons opportunities to sleep cheap, yet spend big. Some of the most elaborate and largest hotels in the world are properties that feature casinos including Las Vegas, Reno, Atlantic City, and many Caribbean islands. Casino hotels can offer low room rates and low food costs because profits are made primarily through

FIGURE 3-3

Mesquite Casino Hotel
Courtesy Las Vegas News Bureau

the gaming. Casino hotels deserve a function category of their own because of their unique characteristics. Casino hotel management is a career field unto itself.

RESORT

Sunning at the beach, skiing, riding horses, physical fitness training, golfing, and playing tennis are but a few of the activities that denote the functions of resorts. They appeal to vacation seekers from all walks of life.

QUALITY RANKING

"We're staying at a four-star hotel," might be heard in conversation. Such a property is quite good, as the highest ranking is usually five stars. Ranking properties can be accomplished by governments, private organizations, or by guide books. The ranking is usually closely tied to price. A one-star ranking is often going to be considered a

budget accommodation. Diamonds, or other such symbols, may be used in place of stars. In words, the rankings might be stated as:

*****	Outstanding, one of the best in the country
****	Excellent, top-quality design and service
***	Very good
**	Good
*	Average

In some countries, the government ranks all hotels as they obtain licensing to operate. Ranking is done through extensive question-naires filled out by trained observers, whose assignment is not known by the establishment being inspected. Each country's ranking criteria is different but in general gives similar guidelines to the traveling public. In many places a property displays the number of stars it has been awarded at its entrance. AAA and Mobil rank hotels in North America. (See Chapter 10, Accommodations: References and Ratings.)

Some guide books use dollar signs to denote price range of a property. These are given specific dollar amounts in a legend explaining the system. Fodor's Travel Guides use this method. Price and quality often go hand-in-hand.

Two additional broad categories can be used in classifying properties: full service and limited service. Full-service properties have door attendants, bellhops, restaurants, bars, room service, and usually shops and a hairdresser. At a limited-service, or self-service, accommodation, guests carry their own bags to their rooms, and a vending machine provides the only food or drink. Obviously most full-service properties are going to be more expensive and have a higher quality ranking than limited-service operations.

OTHER METHODS OF CLASSIFICATION

Though the above classifications overlap, there are yet other rules of thumb that can be used for classification purposes. These include parking facilities, size, affiliation, and clientele.

PARKING FACILITIES

One method of classification is based on the nature of the parking facilities available to guests. A hotel has a garage; a motel has parking right outside the guest room door; and motor inns have parking available in the vicinity of the room.

SIZE

Size is a simple, concrete means of further classifying lodging facilities.

Small—Up to 100 rooms

Medium—100 to 200 rooms

Medium-large—200 to 500 rooms

Large—Over 500 rooms

The size of a hotel/motel makes no difference as to its quality. The Gritti Palace in Venice, Italy, is considered one of the finest hotels in the world. It has only 99 rooms. Some lovely New England inns have only six rooms. Figure 3-4 shows the world's largest hotels.

AFFILIATION

Hotels/motels may be classified as independent or affiliated.

Independents.   Independents are privately owned lodging facilities that have no management alliance with other properties. They have no external criteria to meet with regard to physical, financial, or personnel matters. They may be associated with a hotel representative.

Hotel Representatives.   A ***hotel representative,*** which can be either an individual or a company, works for several independent hotels of the same quality but which do not carry the same name or design. The hotels may be in a variety of locations. The representative might set up a 1-800 telephone number for taking reservations from the public and from one member hotel to another, just like the chains. The representative also does convention promotion work for these hotels, although each is likely to have its own sales/ catering/convention staffs as well.

Chains.   A ***chain*** is an organization of affiliated properties usually bearing the same name, established operating policies, sometimes decor standards, and common reservation systems. Chains have parent-company properties and also may franchise.

A chain searches constantly for potential lucrative locations for parent-company facilities. For example, chains keep abreast of new tourist attractions. An alert chain would have been aware when King's Dominion amusement park was being built in the vicinity north of Richmond, Virginia. The chain would then have proceeded to buy land and build a parent-company facility near this attraction.

Rank	Property Name	Location	Number of Rooms
1	MGM Grand Hotel & Theme Park	Las Vegas	5,005
2	Luxor	Las Vegas	4,467
3	Excalibur	Las Vegas	4,008
4	Circus Circus	Las Vegas	3,744
5	Flamingo Hilton	Las Vegas	3,642
6	Las Vegas Hilton	Las Vegas	3,174
7	Mirage	Las Vegas	3,046
8	Bellagio	Las Vegas	3,005
9	Monte Carlo	Las Vegas	3,002
10	Treasure Island	Las Vegas	2,891
11	Opryland USA	Nashville	2,883
12	Bally's Casino Resort	Las Vegas	2,814
13	Harrah's Las Vegas	Las Vegas	2,700
14	Imperial Palace	Las Vegas	2,700
15	Rio Suite Hotel & Casino	Las Vegas	2,563
16	Hilton Hawaiian Village	Honolulu	2,545
17	Caesars Palace	Las Vegas	2,471
18	Stardust	Las Vegas	2,200
19	New York Hilton	New York	2,131
20	Disney's Caribbean Beach Resort	Orlando	2,112

FIGURE 3-4

Largest hotels in the United States (ranked by Number of Rooms as of December 31, 1998)
Source: Las Vegas Convention & Visitors Authority

A second way that chain affiliations are made is through *franchises.* Developers in a particular area agree on a location, pool their finances, and decide to build a hotel. They search for a nationally known franchised lodging chain that agrees with their plans and will take over the management of that hotel. The chain might control the architecture, interior design, purchasing, personnel, advertising, and central reservation network.

We are all familiar with the large chains that dot the landscape of the United States: Holiday Inn, Ramada Inn, Marriott, Hilton; the list could go on and on.

When hotel/motels are members of a chain they often share operating policies and reservation systems.

CLIENTELE

Though type of traveler is discussed somewhat under extended-stay properties, within the function classification, a broader way to categorize lodgings is that they may appeal to and cater to either transient or residential clientele or both. The ***transient clients*** may be vacation travelers or business travelers. Business travel makes up the largest portion of the hotel business in most large cities. A beach town, on the other hand, would have hotels that appeal to vacation travelers.

Residential clients lease rooms at hotels with weekly or monthly rates. Often these are elderly people who want the convenience of a downtown location. In large cities, social services may contract for a number of units in order to place homeless people there in emergencies. Sometimes the poor pool their resources to rent rooms. Many large corporations maintain two or three rooms in a hotel in a large city and pay a monthly or yearly rate. They know that their

salespeople fill these rooms often enough to make it economical for them to rent on a long-term basis, even though their rooms might be empty on weekends.

TRENDS

Branding has been a phenomena for the last two decades and will continue to be so. The term is used when a hospitality company owns or franchises several types of lodgings that are given different names, which could be called brands. For example, there are Marriott Hotels, Residence Inns, and Courtyard by Marriott. Each is different in design and service, but all take advantage of the Marriott name recognition and corporate support.

The advantages of branding lie primarily with being able to segment the market. Different travelers have different needs. One needs a full-service hotel for one night, while the other needs extended-stay accommodations. Branding permits advertising to target specific markets. It also permits travelers to identify with and choose the precise type of accommodations that they prefer.

Large hotel companies are buying multiple chains causing major consolidations in the industry. In many instances this allows for improvements in personnel management and purchasing. It also presents opportunities for international expansion. Though two companies that currently own multiple brands have familiar names, Hilton and Marriott, others are not so familiar. For example, Promus Hotels Corporation owns Doubletree, Homewood Suites, Embassy Suites, and Hampton Inn brands. Carlson Hospitality, Patriot American, Starwood Lodging, and Cendant Corporation are other such companies. It has been predicted that in the next century half a dozen companies will own the majority of hotel chains.

The number of all-suite lodgings, which emerged in the 1980s, will continue to grow as even leisure travelers enjoy the amenities of a kitchen and sitting room. On the other hand, B & Bs will also increase, as leisure travelers seek more personal atmospheres and people contact. The trend of building properties with thousands of rooms will continue at some locations. The number of properties and total room count worldwide will continue to increase as both business and leisure travel grow, in particular as international travel becomes more commonplace.

> For the purpose of this text the terms *hotel* and *motel* are used interchangeably to cover all classifications of lodging facilities.

CHAPTER ACTIVITIES

1. Place the following words in the classification system where they might be used. Some may be included in more than one classification.

hotel	airport	convention	casino
condo	resort	extended stay	motor inn
B & B	time-share	motel	commercial

   FUNCTION   TERMINOLOGY   LOCATION

2. List and define five vocabulary words used in this chapter.

   A.

   B.

   C.

   D.

   E.

CHAPTER PROJECTS

CLASSIFICATION OF LODGING FACILITIES

1. Ask three friends or family members to define *hotel* and *motel*. Tell the class what differences they pointed out.

2. List the nationally known chains represented by hotel/motels in your area.

3. Visit a chain hotel/motel in your area and find out how this affiliation came about. Explain your findings in a paragraph.

4. Interview someone who has stayed at a resort in the United States, a bed and breakfast in the United Kingdom, or a pensione in Europe. Tell the class the person's impressions.

4

FRONT-OFFICE OPERATIONS:
RESERVATIONS

CHAPTER OUTLINE

I. *The Front Office*
   Personnel
   Organization
II. *Selling Rooms*
   Pricing Rooms
   Yield Management
III. *Processing Reservations*
   Type of Reservation
   Source of Reservations
   Processing Reservations

LEARNING OBJECTIVES

After reading this chapter, you should be able to

- Distinguish between the different types of rooms in a hotel/motel.
- Describe the criteria for pricing rooms.
- Understand yield management concepts.
- Trace what happens to a hotel reservation from its receipt to the guest's arrival.
- Complete reservation and confirmation forms.

THE FRONT OFFICE

The *front office* of a hotel/motel generally performs the following 10 basic activities:

1. Processing advance reservations
2. Registering guests
3. Rooming guests
4. Moving guests' luggage
5. Issuing room keys
6. Providing information
7. Handling guests' mail
8. Administering telephone service
9. Accounting (making payments and billing)
10. Checking out guests

This chapter covers processing advance reservations and registering guests. Chapter 5 covers rooming guests, issuing room keys, moving guests' luggage, providing information, receiving and delivering mail, and administering telephone service. Chapter 6 covers accounting and checking out guests.

PERSONNEL

The front office is the nerve center of any hotel operation. Hotel personnel are there to serve guests. An important aspect of this is providing a good first impression of the establishment to guests. Many people are involved in serving guests: reservation clerks, front-desk clerks, room clerks, key clerks, and mail clerks. These titles are often interchangeable depending on the size and nature of the organization. Chapter 2 describes service as it applies to hotel/motel operations.

ORGANIZATION

In a small hotel there may be no difference between the front desk or rooms division and the front office. Larger establishments have a front office with a manager who supervises the front desk. A front-office organization in a large hotel usually includes the front desk, uniformed services, the switchboard, reservations, and possibly

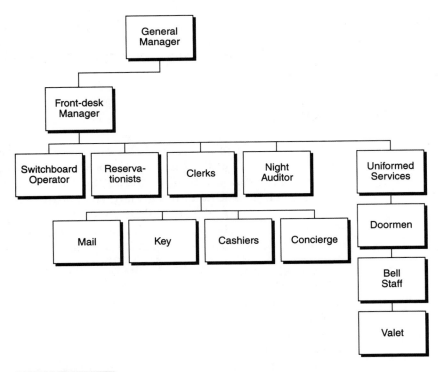

Organization chart for a 500-room full-service hotel

housekeeping. The nature of the front-desk operation depends on the size of the lodging.

In a large hotel the accounting department might fall under direction of the *controller,* who reports to the general manager. In a smaller hotel the accounting department may be under the front office. Figure 4-1 shows an organization chart possible for front-desk operations for a 500-room establishment.

The physical appearance of a front office varies from large to small, full-service to limited-service, and exclusive to budget properties. The front desk is usually a counter located in the lobby. The size and decor of lobbies differs greatly. The reservations office is often not seen, but is in close proximity to the front desk. People who fill many of the positions shown in the organization chart are stationed behind the front-desk counter. The concierge usually occupies a small counter desk or regular office desk elsewhere in the lobby. Bellhops usually have a stand near the door.

SELLING ROOMS

The front office has two aims and responsibilities: selling rooms and serving guests.

PRICING ROOMS

The first aim or responsibility of the front office is to sell all available rooms in the hotel at the highest rate possible. Obviously, it is preferable to sell a room at a double rate rather than at a single rate. Each room is given a *rack rate* or standard *room rate,* but that is not necessarily the rate at which it will be sold. Front-desk personnel don't set room rates, but they need to know how the rates are derived.

Room rates are usually determined using the following criteria:

1. Type of room
2. Location of room
3. Season and seasonal events
4. Kind of guest
5. Meal plan
6. Length of stay
7. Day of the week

1. Type of Room.   The terminology may vary with the establishment, but basically the phrase "type of room" denotes the size or number of people a room will accommodate. Most guests will request a single or double room, and rates are based on such. From that point, bed-size preference is stated. The rate charged for two people in a double room is higher than that for one person, even though the single person may be placed in a room with a double bed. A charge is sometimes imposed for *EAP,* "each additional person." The classifications overlap and thus can be quite confusing. Following are the basic classifications:

Single room—A room that can accommodate and is sold to only one person. It might have any combination of single, double, and queen-size beds in it.

Double room—A room that can accommodate two people in a double or queen-size bed.

Twin double room (also double-double room or queen double)— A room with two twin, double, or queen beds that can accommodate two to four people. We often see two double beds in the larger motor inns. Few properties have twin beds.

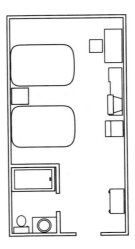

Triple room—A room that can accommodate three people either in one double bed and one twin bed, in three twin beds, or in two double beds. A triple rate might be charged if a cot is brought into a double or twin double. Often there is no charge if the cot is for a child.

Quad—A room that can accommodate four people in twin or double beds.

Suite—A guest space that contains one or more bedrooms. The bedrooms may be singles, doubles, or twin doubles.

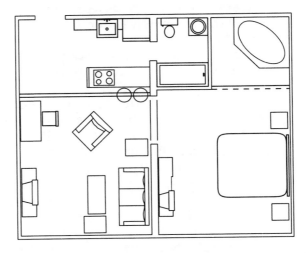

Connecting rooms—Two rooms located side by side with a door between the two.

Adjacent or **adjoining rooms**—Rooms located side by side that do not necessarily have a connecting door.

Occasionally abbreviations are used for these various types of rooms. *S* would be single, and *DD* would be double-double. In some countries abbreviations such as *SWB* and *DWB* are still in use. These denote single-with-bath and double-with-bath.

Other types of rooms include nonsmoking and handicapped accessible. Usually there is no extra charge for these.

2. Location of Room.   Preferable room locations within a hotel are those with picturesque, poolside, or seaside views. Rooms in these locations usually are more expensive than identical rooms in other locations. In hotels located in the city the rooms on the lower floors often are less expensive because of noise from outside traffic. Rooms near high-traffic areas within the hotel complex, such as elevators or soft drink and ice machines, are also often discounted.

A recent innovation in hotels is the ***tower concept.*** These are rooms which are usually on the top floors of a property designated for VIPs. An elevator key must be used to reach these floors. Special hotel personnel are assigned to serve these rooms, and often there are special registration desks. This special treatment is called ***concierge service*** and might even include cocktails and breakfast served in luxurious lounges. Needless to say, these rooms are priced more expensively than others in the hotel.

Tour operators and conference managers who block multiple rooms at a property usually book ***ROH*** or run-of-the-house. This means members of the group may be roomed at any location of the hotel.

3. Season and Seasonal Events.   Certainly in many resort hotels the rates change according to the season or the area's most popular tourist time. Prices on a Caribbean island are higher in winter when people seek the sun. By the same token, when there is a good snow cover, ski resorts can demand higher prices. Seasonal events, such as the Kentucky Derby, the Indianapolis 500, or spring break in Panama City, Florida, or Cancun, Mexico, cause all rooms in the vicinity to be sold at premium prices for the duration of these events.

4. Kind of Guest.   The majority of guests receive the standard rate. Some large companies and the government receive a commercial or "corporate" rate for their employees. This is somewhat lower than the standard rate. A company might qualify for a discount because of the quantity of business it annually sends to the individual hotel/motel

or chain. Conference attendees generally receive reduced rates that a meeting planner has negotiated with the hotel because of the volume of guests being booked. The same is true for those on tours, where group rates were contracted by the tour operator or travel agent. Some properties have higher charges for their office-equipped rooms for business travelers. A $15 surcharge may be added to the bill to assure such amenities as the latest in modem connections, free local telephone calls, and credit card direct phoning. Certain VIPs, airline personnel, travel agents, and employees of the hotel system or chain get a reduced rate or possibly "complimentary" (no charge) room rates. "Children Stay Free" is advertised by some chains, particularly Holiday Inn.

Members of certain organizations have negotiated discounts at major hospitality chains. The American Automobile Association (AAA) and American Association of Retired People (AARP) are examples. Usually set reductions, such as 5 or 10 percent discounts, are applied to the price discussed. Members of a chain's frequent-user program can receive free or discounted rates. Each night's stay at a chain-affiliated property awards points toward free or discounted room-nights.

5. Meal Plan. Some hotels, primarily in the resort category, offer meals included in the price of the room. The plans are as follows:

AP **American Plan**—All meals included

MAP **Modified American Plan**—Breakfast and lunch or dinner included

CP **Continental Plan**—Breakfast included (usually not a full breakfast)

BP **Bermuda Plan**—Full breakfast included

EP **European Plan**—No meals included

The concept of **all-inclusive** resorts and vacations has grown tremendously in the past decade. One price includes hotel room, all meals, beverages, recreational fees, and usually transportation costs. The vacationer has pre-paid all except discriminatory expenses.

6. Length of Stay. Resident guests stay at a hotel for an extended length of time, thereby qualifying for a reduced room rate. As has been previously discussed, extended-stay, residence hotels, and all-suite properties are among the fastest growing trends in the lodging industry. Companies may also rent a room or rooms annually for

365 nights of the year and thereby get a reduced rate. One particularly nice hotel in New York rents suites to employees of the United Nations at an annual rate. The United Nations employees occupy these rooms Monday through Thursday nights, then the hotel offers these suites to the public on weekends at very reasonable prices. Some properties will rent a room at a lower day rate if it is vacated by 5 or 6 o'clock so it can be rented that night.

7. Day of the Week.   From the above example you see that the day of the week can make a difference in room price. Most hotels in the city cater primarily to business travelers. On weekends their occupancy rates are lower, so the hotel is willing to lower room rates. A recent call to a Washington, D.C., chain motel, requesting a room for two nights, Thursday and Friday, resulted in a price quote of $139 per night. The caller's comment "But, Friday is a weekend night; isn't that rate lower?" resulted in a $99 room rate for Friday.

The many variances in room rates can cause confusion among guests. In casual poolside conversation, a 50 percent difference in rate may be discovered by a guest. For instance one person might have a weekend rate and another may not. If this discrepancy is questioned, the front-desk manager will usually allow the lower rate.

YIELD MANAGEMENT

Hotel rates must be high enough to cover operating expenses, debt, and profits expected by owners. On the other hand, they must be low enough to attract guests. A hotel room is considered a perishable product. If it is not used and thereby not paid for on any night, that income is lost.

The term *yield management* basically refers to calculations that lead to maximizing the amount of income or revenue from room sales. To do this, maximum room rates and occupancy rates are needed to produce higher daily averages. Complicated formulas and computer programs assist a hotel manager or the comptroller to adjust room rates to optimize room sales profits on any given day, virtually at any given time of day.

In addition to the concrete criteria discussed previously about pricing rooms, other factors also apply. The status of the property, be it economy or luxury, its determined break-even point, and its location and price as compared to competition also come into play to formulate the rack price. Many properties change such rates often. They may be juggled upward or down in the effort to maximize revenue.

Rates are usually advertised "subject to availability" to allow flexibility. Chapter 10 shows that a range of prices is quoted in reference materials, thus allowing for such price changes.

Occupancy rates, which are used to formulate forecasts, are the tools of yield management. *Occupancy rates* are derived from dividing the number of rooms available for rent into the number of rooms occupied. For example 100 rooms available, divided into 70 rooms rented, equals a 70 percent occupancy rate. This must be established in order to create *forecasts*, which are estimates of the number of guests/rooms populated, thus occupancy rates for the future. A forecast is formulated by taking historic occupancy figures over several years and adding new data, such as physical improvements, event occurrences, and intensified advertising campaigns. Projected occupancy can then be forecasted, and if lower than desired, rate changes can be made to fill more hotel rooms.

Room rate changes may be made on an annual basis. For example, raising corporate and government rates when annual occupancy percentages are expected to rise may occur. Convention and tour group rates may be changed according to projected occupancy rates in a given time frame.

Other considerations that may be accounted for in yield management are the percentage of double- versus single-room sales and commissions paid to travel agent bookings. *Nonrevenue* (nonrev) rooms, which are free or complimentary, must be included in formulas. These may be occupied by conference planners or frequent-user program guests.

On the short-term side, a 10-day or 3-day forecast enables the front-desk manager to adjust prices. On a daily basis the front desk might be alerted to reduce rates to walk-ins when occupancy is lower than expected. Forecasts enable the front-desk manager to notify other departments, such as housekeeping and food and beverage for staffing and purchasing.

Yield management systems allow rates to vary continually according to supply and demand. The purpose is to maximize profits. Airlines use the same theory in setting their multileveled fares.

Figure 4-2 shows selected cities across the United States that reflect highest and lowest average room rates.

PROCESSING RESERVATIONS

Reservations are received by the hotel possibly one hour in advance, or on the part of conferences possibly years in advance.

Highest Average Room Rates of Selected Citites	
New York, NY	$168.33
New Orleans, LA	123.98
San Francisco, CA	118.09
Boston, MA	116.01
Honolulu, HI	111.52
Charleston, SC	103.67
Baltimore, MD	102.82
San Antonio, TX	102.11
Chicago, IL	101.39
West Palm Beach, FL	100.18
Lowest Average Room Rates of Selected Cities	
Bismark, ND	$ 42.81
Las Cruces, NM	44.01
Billings, MT	45.10
Sioux Falls, SD	47.64
Reno, NV	50.95
Jackson, MS	51.53
Little Rock, AK	51.89
Charleston, WV	52.57
Oklahoma City, OK	52.75
La Crosse, WI	53.98

FIGURE 4-2

Sample room rates.
Source: American Hotel Foundation, 1999.

TYPE OF RESERVATION

There are two basic types of reservations, regular or guaranteed. A *regular reservation* or nonguaranteed reservation is not paid in advance and the room is held until a specified time (usually 6 P.M.) on the date of arrival. If the guest does not arrive by the specified time, the reservation is released and the room is sold to a **walk-in** (a person with no reservation who appears at a property desiring a room). To secure a *guaranteed reservation,* the client pays for the first night prior to his or her arrival. This may be in the form of a credit card number or receipt of the first day's payment. Guaranteed reservations are essential for late arrivals, when guests know they will arrive after the specified

time. A guaranteed room is usually held until checkout time the following day.

SOURCE OF RESERVATIONS

Sources of reservations include reservation centers, property-to-property, third parties, and direct. Technology allows thousands of property chains to have a central reservation center situated at one location. To reserve a room in Paris, a person might speak with someone in North Dakota. Computers and 1-800/1-888 telephone numbers convey reservation demands and confirmations to the chain's establishments all over the world. Through the same technology a chain-affiliated property in one city can contact another affiliate elsewhere to conclude property-to-property reservations.

Third parties make reservations for individuals or groups. Hotel representatives serving independent hotels have reservation centers that book rooms. Travel agents reserve rooms for clients. In both of these incidences, fees or commissions are paid by the lodging establishment. Tour operators make group bookings for their tour participants, as do meeting planners reserving multiple rooms for their conference attendees.

Direct reservations are made by individuals who book rooms personally with the property. The reservation method used may be via mail, telephone, fax, e-mail, through a Web site, or face to face.

PROCESSING RESERVATIONS

Upon receiving a reservation request, the reservation clerk checks the availability of rooms on the dates requested. A computer can show the availability of different types of rooms for any given date. Figure 4-3 is a standard computer printout showing the types of rooms and the number available for each day of the week. The computer can give space availability for years in advance. The reservation clerk keys in the new reservation and the computer reflects one less room available.

Figure 4-4 shows a handwritten availability chart which demonstrates the basis of the computer printout. Note that the chart covers an entire month. Counting backwards, crossing off figures as reservations are received shows the number of rooms yet available. Note that this chart covers an entire month. The numbers do not indicate room numbers but only show how many rooms are available. Reservations might also be posted by hand in a calendar-type book.

JUL--				ROOM AVAILABILITY				07/16/--		09:28
	15	16	17	18	19	20	21	22	23	24
	FRI	SAT	SUN	MON	TUE	WED	THU	FRI	SAT	SUN
STND	85	114	94	45	47	101	80	42	110	103
KING	24	36	30	55	53	47	32	51	37	50
ESPC	2	1	1	3	3	4	2	4	1	2
HAND	2	3	2	0	0	2	3	2	4	2
EKTC	3	1	2	0	0	2	2	1	1	2
EPAR	1	1	1	1	1	1	1	1	1	1
EBDL	1	1	1	1	1	0	0	1	1	1
KNSM	8	7	6	7	8	7	2	2	7	6
SNSM	8	9	6	8	7	9	2	3	9	3
ENSM	2	2	2	2	2	1	2	2	2	1
BEDDED	77	38	68	91	91	39	26	104	40	42
% OCC.	36	18	32	43	43	18	12	49	19	20
HOS	1	1	1	1	1	1	1	1	1	1
PERM	8	8	8	8	8	8	8	8	8	8

FIGURE 4-3

Availability printout for a computerized system

Primary information taken for a reservation, be it handwritten or computer, is the name, address, and phone number of the guest, type of room, date and time of arrival, number of nights, number in party, rate established, and method of payment. Special requests such as an infant crib or a cot also are noted and reserved. No matter which reservation system is used, this basic information is required.

It is most important that a record be kept of who made the reservation. Sometimes this might be a travel agent whereby the company name should be recorded. Any changes should be made promptly, and who made the change should be noted.

Often advance payments, either checks or credit card authorization, are included with the reservation. A record of this **PIA (Paid in Advance)** is kept and transferred to the guest's folio upon arrival. The reservation is flagged as guaranteed.

Upon receiving a reservation the clerk fills out a reservation card in duplicate as shown handwritten in Figure 4-5. Such cards are then filed in a rack or box. The cards are filed by date of arrival and in alphabetical order by name of guest. At the beginning of

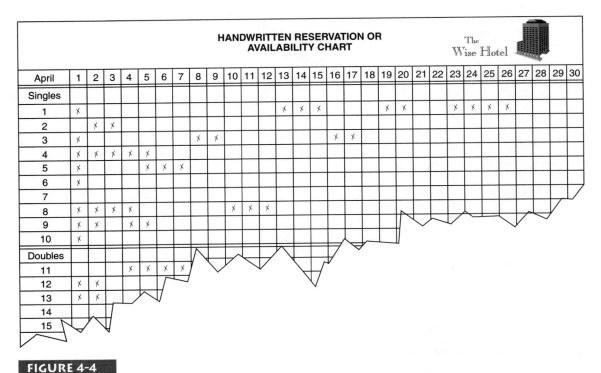

FIGURE 4-4

Handwritten reservation or availability chart

each month, that month's reservations are placed in the current section of the box or chart. More often, the same information is typed into a database form on a computer. Special requests, such as handicapped accessible, poolside, or connecting rooms, must be prominently noted. Rooms that satisfy such guest's needs are often blocked at this time. The reservation information can be retrieved by entering a guest's name, or the computer can display reservations by date.

Group reservations may come in from a tour operator or for a convention months or even years in advance. For such advance reservations, there would be no names, but the reservations chart or file would reflect how many rooms, often on the same floor, are **blocked rooms.** These rooms are often sold at a discounted room rate by the hotel's group sales department. The organization holding the convention might send out a reservation card that the attendee would mail directly to the hotel/motel. Or the organization itself could receive reservations and communicate periodically with the hotel concerning the number of rooms needed for the event.

The Wise Hotel

RESERVATION CARD

RESERVATION NUMBER _98703_

ARRIVAL _September 3, 20--_   RESERVATION DATE _Aug. 27, 20--_

DEPARTURE _September 5, 20--_   VIA _phone_

NUMBER OF GUESTS _2_   AGENT _____

TYPE OF ROOM _twin_   CONFIRMED _____

RATE _$72 per night_   GUARANTEED _✓_

NAME _Ms. Jean Jennings_

ADDRESS _6918 Wynne Court_

Augusta, Georgia 30813-1024

COMPANY _Lyon Chemicals, Inc._

WORK PHONE _404-555-2353_   HOME PHONE _404-555-1111_

METHOD OF PAYMENT _Plus credit card_   CLERK: _____

FIGURE 4-5

Registration card for a noncomputerized operation

Canceling Reservations. Travelers are doing a hotel a favor by letting it know if they do not plan to use a reservation. The cancellation frees the room to be re-rented. For this reason reservation clerks should express extreme courtesy when taking the cancellation. Cancellation numbers should be given to each such transaction. The number is usually composed of date (Julian dates are most often used), property ID number, consecutive number of cancellations in the year, and initials of the person taking the cancellation.

With nonguaranteed reservations the clerk pulls the reservation card or retrieves the guest's name in the computer reservation data bank. Then the type room reserved is placed back into the available room pool. With guaranteed reservations the same process is followed, but the deposit must be returned or credited. Each chain or property has a cancellation policy. It is wise to have it stated on the confirmation card as shown on Figure 4-6. There are legal issues con-

Confirmation Printout

Gateway
Resort

John Wren
123 Westbard Ave.
Garliss, NC 01234
(999)123-4567

Check-in Time: 5:00 p.m.
Check-out Time: 11:00 a.m.

CONFIRMATION

CONFIRMATION NO.	NUMBER OF ROOMS	ARRIVAL STATUS	GUESTS	RATES	GUARANTEED	ADVANCE DEPOSIT
10076B35	1	PM	2	98.00	PLUS	98.00

RESERVED ON	ARRIVAL DATE	DEPARTURE DATE	ROOM TYPE REQUESTED		MEMBER
9/7/- -	9/10/- -.	9/12/- -	DBL — DBL		NO

CREDIT TO BE ESTABLISHED PRIOR TO OR AT REGISTRATION

If you find it necessary to cancel this reservation, please call 1-800-123-4567. Room reservations will be held until 5:00 p.m. on the date of arrival. All pre-paid reservation cancellations should be received 24 hours prior to the date of arrival for a refund to be issued.

FIGURE 4-6

Confirmation printout

cerning refunds of advance payment if it was charged to a credit card. As a cross-check, a daily log can be kept, listing chronologically all cancellations.

Confirming Reservations. If time allows, the hotel should confirm the reservation, preferably in writing, though it may be confirmed in the way in which it was received, via phone, e-mail, fax, or letter. Of course, on computer systems, a confirmation printout like the one in Figure 4-6 will be made. This is sent to the guest immediately. A standard confirmation form is often used or, if more personal confirmations are desired, a form letter may be used. The personalized confirmation letter shown in Figure 4-7 shows an example of this. Confirmation numbers are given.

If payment for the room is not received in advance, the clerk notes on the reservation card the room rate quoted, amount due, and the time limit for which the reservation will be held. Unless there is a special request, rooms are not usually assigned until the day of the guest's arrival.

The
Wise Hotel

(DATE)

(NAME)
(ADDRESS)
(CITY, STATE, AND ZIP CODE)

Dear (NAME):

Thank you for your reservation. We look
forward to providing you with excellent accommodations and service.

We have reserved for you: (NUMBER) (TYPE) rooms
for (NUMBER) persons for (NUMBER) nights, from
(DATE) to (DATE).

Remember that we cannot hold your reservation
later than 6:00 p.m. unless it is paid for in
advance.

Your confirmation number is: (NUMBER).

We look forward to seeing you at the WISE
Hotel.

Sincerely,

(RESERVATION MANAGER'S NAME)
Reservation Manager

FIGURE 4-7

Personalized confirmation letter

Checking Daily Reservations. Each morning the room clerk obtains
the day's reservations from the computer reservations box, or chart.
The clerk would take note of type, rate, special requests, and whether
a reservation is guaranteed. The reservation might be assigned with
an appropriate room number. A room registration hold sheet, as
shown in Figure 4-8, might be used for this purpose. Computers allow

ROOM REGISTRATION HOLD SHEET

DATE _February 3,_ _____20 __ _____   DAY _Sunday_ _____

	LETTER	1-800	PHONE	IN PERSON	RESERVATION NUMBER	NAME	GUARANTEED YES	GUARANTEED NO	NUMBER IN PARTY	KIND OF ROOM	RATE	ROOM ASSIGN-MENT
1			✓			Sally Logan	✓		1	SWB	$57.00	203
						712-555-2312 Council Bluffs, IA						
2	✓					Mr. & Mrs. J. Briggs		✓	2	DWB	$73.	421
						406-555-2396 Billings, MT						
3	✓					Ms. R. Lind	✓		1	SWB	$57.00	242
						207-555-6616 Augusta, ME						
4												

FIGURE 4-8

Room registration hold sheet

front-desk clerks to assign rooms to guests when they arrive. This presents the opportunity to sell up or more properly serve the guest.

In the past a ***room board,*** sometimes called a ***room rack,*** was used. A few smaller properties still use these.

Room boards are usually seen behind the front desk. On the room board, room numbers are beside slots where the status of the room can be shown. Occupied rooms are indicated by inserting a copy of the registration slip in the corresponding slot. On the sample room board illustrated in Figure 4-9, you can see that Room 101 is an available double room. The $85–92 rate for Room 101 is dependent on the number of people occupying it and whether a discounted rate applies. The board further indicates that Room 102 is a single with a $75–85 rate. In addition, the plastic covering over 104 and 202 indicates that these rooms are being cleaned (***OC*** or ***on change***). Rooms 105, 203, 204, and 205 are blocked for guests arriving that day.

Computers have revolutionized reservations and check-in. With a few keyboard commands the reservationist can show the rooms available and can check a list of arrivals, as shown in Figure 4-10. The desk clerk can assign rooms almost instantaneously. Computers show rooms

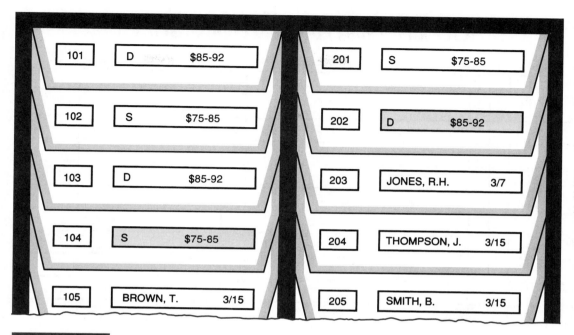

Room board

on change, **OOO (out of order),** and **sleepers** (rooms that are vacant and ready for occupancy but through some error do not appear available on the room list or computer). Sleepers result in a loss of revenue.

Other room situations that might show on the computer are **stayovers** or **overstays**—persons staying longer than the length of their reservation; **due-outs**—those who are due to check out; and **sleptouts**—people who paid for the room but did not sleep there. Sleptouts occur often when a person is on a package tour, has prepaid for six nights, but vacations elsewhere for a few of those days. Some computers show the following terms: **DNS (did not stay), DNA (did not arrive),** or **RNA (registered but not assigned).** All of these figures compiled are used in forecasts and yield management.

TRENDS

E-mail is rapidly becoming the most popular reservation communication method, as even small properties are going on-line. Making hotel reservations via the Internet while in-flight to a destination will

ARRIVALS REPORT FOR 04/27/--

04/27/-- 12:13:56

1-GATEWAY RESORT

ROOM	CM	#RM	ACCT#	S	PLAN	ARRIVAL	DEPART	GUEST NAME	FIRM NAME	CONF NO.	SPECIAL REQU
KING	1	1	5043		9	04/27/--	04/30/--	KENNEDY/KEVIN	FORRESTER PUMPS INC	71903LAK	
DBDB	1	1	5044	s	6	04/27/--	04/30/--	MCNAIR/ROBERT	CONSOLIDATED MINES	724748AK	SIGN RM&TAX
DBDB	1	1	5045	s	5	04/27/--	04/30/--	PRIESTLY/GREGORY	CONSOLIDATED MINES	724748AK	SIGN RM&TAX
KING	1	1	5046		9	04/27/--	04/30/--	DENNIS/JOSEPH	IAFF	726L53AK	
DBDB	1	1	5048		9	04/27/--	04/30/--	SMITH/JAMES	IAFF	724J2AK	
DBDB	1	1	5049		9	04/27/--	05/01/--	BARLAER/WHITT	IAFF	776W53AK	
KING	1	1	5122		9	04/27/--	04/30/--	FRANKEL/STAN	IAFF	728J20AK	
KING	1	1	5053		9	04/27/--	04/28/--	KERK/GLORIA	PIEDMONT AIRLINES	778977AK	SPLIT RES
KING	1	1	5056		9	04/27/--	04/28/--	RANDALL/TOM	PIEDMONT AIRLINES	78J1HQAK	SPLIT RES
KING	1	1	4878		6	04/27/--	04/28/--	ROBINSON/MARTY	T.W.A. AIRLINES	76HJ46AK	
KING	1	1	4879		9	04/27/--	04/29/--	BEELS/DONOVAN	SAVE-ALL	76259PLAK	
KING	1	1	5063		9	04/27/--	04/30/--	PAUL/MARY	AMERICAN COAL	738HLHAK	
DBDB	1	1	5064		9	04/27/--	04/28/--	SKYLES/THOMAS	T.W.A. AIRLINES	77HX9HAK	
DBDB	1	1	5065		9	04/27/--	04/28/--	RUIZ / MERCEDES	UNITED COAL	750718AK	
DBDB	1	1	5134		6	04/27/--	04/30/--	MCCARTNEY/PETE	APPLETON RECORDING, INC.	760Q00AK	
DBDB	1	1	5067		9	04/27/--	04/28/--	STARKEY/RENE	APPLETON RECORDING, INC.	71846QAK	
KING	1	1	5136		9	04/27/--	04/28/--	LENNON/JANE	CHALLIS READYWEAR	750790AK	
DBDB	1	1	4899		9	04/27/--	05/01/--	HARRISON/GLORIA	CHILIDOG RESTAURANTS	7232JWAK	
KING	1	1	4900		9	04/27/--	04/29/--	CAMPBELL/GLENNA	UNIVERSITY OF CINCINNATI	7076W3AK	
DBDB	1	1	5072		9	04/27/--	04/28/--	MILLER/GEORGIA	UNIVERSITY OF CINCINNATI	7159W9AK	
KING	1	1	5073		9	04/27/--	04/30/--	SCHROEDER/GERALDINE	T.W.A.AIRLINES	763181AK	
DBDB	1	1	5074		6	04/27/--	04/30/--	EVERLEY/MARY MARGARET	COAL COMPANIES OF PENNSYLVANIA	760X36AK	
DBDB	1	1	4796		9	04/27/--	04/30/--	ROGERS/PETER	ENTERPRISE, INC.	724938AK	
KING	1	1	5076		9	04/27/--	04/30/--	MELENDEZ/AMELIA	MIDWESTERN FARMS, INC.	728J33AK	
DBDB	1	1	5077		9	04/27/--	05/01/--	HOLLIS/BRENDA	KEILOR, INC.	75XJ26AK	
KING	1	1	5078		9	04/27/--	04/28/--	DAY/JENNA	KEILOR, INC.	715927AK	
DBDB	1	1	4909		9	04/27/--	04/30/--	KNIGHT/BARBARA	CHAMPION SAVINGS	778758AK	
DBDB	1	1	4910		9	04/27/--	04/30/--	ADAMS/JOANNA	PAPER MANUFACTURERS OF AMERICA	74W702AK	
KING	1	1	4808		9	04/27/--	04/29/--	AUSTIN/BRETT	IAFF	738Q03AK	
KING	1	1	5083		9	04/27/--	04/30/--	BERRY/ALAN	UNIVERSITY OF CINCINNATI	727J46AK	
KING	1	1	5084		9	04/27/--	04/30/--	YI/YANG	WEDDING CONSULTANTS, INC.	750923AK	
KING	1	1	5085		9	04/27/--	04/29/--	CONNAIR/PETER	IBM	7884H1AK	
KING	1	1	5086		9	04/27/--	04/30/--	CONDOR/JOE	WEDDING CONSULTANTS, INC.	73HQH9AK	
DBDB	1	1	5087		9	04/27/--	05/01/--	CONWAY/CAROL	HOME CITY SAVINGS	78X2J4AK	
DBDB	1	1	5088		9	04/27/--	04/30/--	MARVIN/W.	ATLANTIC INDEMNITY	74J379AK	
KING	1	1	4923		9	04/27/--	04/30/--	PETERO/JOYCE	KEILOR, INC.	7666C6AK	
DBDB	1	1	5090		9	04/27/--	05/01/--	SHAW/JOHN	SUPREME CANDY, INC.	76J27LAK	
DBDB	1	1	5091		9	04/27/--	04/28/--	ROSS/DEBORAH	PRODUCTIONS, INC.	78Q6XAK	
KING	1	1	5092		9	04/27/--	04/30/--	LUCCI/SHARON	UNIVERSITY OF CINCINNATI	76504LAK	
DBDB	1	1	5094		9	04/27/--	04/30/--	OCONNOR/SHARON	COAL COMPANIES OF PENNSYLVANIA		
DBDB	1	1	5095		9	04/27/--	04/30/--	BROWN/BONITA	IAFF	728J09AK	
KING	1	1	5096		9	04/27/--	04/28/--	MILEY/ROBERT	PRODUCTIONS, INC.	723307AK	
KING	1	1	4932		9	04/27/--	04/30/--	JOHNSON/CARL	CHAMPION SAVINGS		
KING	1	1	5098		9	04/27/--	05/01/--	PEREZ/ADA	PAPER MANUFACTURERS OF AMERICA	772164AK	
DBDB	1	1	5099		9	04/27/--	04/29/--	GINN/BARBARA	PRODUCTIONS, INC.	723768AK	
KING	1	1	5100		9	04/27/--	04/28/--	RAMSDELL/CAROLINE	UNITED COAL	715L63AK	
KING	1	1	4939		9	04/27/--	04/28/--	JACKSON/CLYDE	KNIGHT COAL	7705Q8AK	
DBDB	1	1	4941	s	9	04/27/--	04/30/--	HILDEBRAND/CHARLES	ENTERPRISE, INC.	7788LJAK	SIGN RM&TAX
DBDB	1	1	5103		9	04/27/--	04/28/--	HUGHES/W.E.	APPLETON RECORDING, INC.	724773AK	
KING	1	1	5105		9	04/27/--	04/30/--	KRAMER/DAVE	SHIRTS UNLIMITED	76LQH3AK	
DBDB	1	1	5106		9	04/27/--	05/01/--	KINNEY/DORCHESTER	SAVE-ALL	750420AK	
DBDB	1	1	5107		9	04/27/--	04/30/--	KUSNERAK/KAREN	SAVE-ALL	78W75AK	
KING	1	1	5108		9	04/27/--	05/01/--	CORKEN/ALAN	SAVE-ALL	750H64AK	

FIGURE 4-10

Arrivals report

69

become more feasible. Computer technology allows travelers to fill out reservation cards from their home or office in many cases. Faxing reservations and confirmations is more and more popular, particularly when dealing with overseas countries and the subsequent time zone changes.

In the future, computer programs will become more sophisticated. These will more accurately analyze reservation demands and will allow for more accurate forecasts. As the number of variables that can be inserted into forecast formulas increases, so will its reliability increase.

With the "shrinking world" phenomena and international travel increasing, reservation telephone clerks with language capabilities will be in more demand. In addition, an ever increasing pool of on-call translators for written reservations in other languages will be needed.

CHAPTER ACTIVITIES

FRONT-OFFICE OPERATIONS: RESERVATIONS

1. Fill out the reservation card below according to the following letter the hotel received:

WILLIAM S. PAGE

March 12, 19--

The Wise Hotel
123 Berwinkle Boulevard
Los Angeles, CA 90077-1024

Dear Sirs:

My wife and I will be arriving in Los Angeles
on April 1 and will stay through April 5.
We would like a room with twin beds in the
range of $40-60 per night. Please reserve a
room for us. We will be paying on Plus Credit
Card #123-456-78.

Sincerely,

Bill Page
1234 Bower Street
Cincinnati, OH 45211-4613

The
Wise Hotel

RESERVATION CARD

RESERVATION NUMBER _____

ARRIVAL _____

RESERVATION DATE _____

DEPARTURE _____

VIA _____

NUMBER OF GUESTS_____

AGENT _____

TYPE OF ROOM _____

CONFIRMED_____

RATE _____

GUARANTEED _____

NAME _____

ADDRESS _____

_____

COMPANY _____

WORK PHONE _____

HOME PHONE _____

METHOD OF PAYMENT _____

2. Name four front-office positions and write a five-sentence job
   description for each.

3. Draw a line between the abbreviations and terms and their
   correct definitions:

EAP	A room that is being cleaned
sleeper	A guest who pays for a room, but does not use it to sleep
DD	A guest who stays longer than her reservation indicated
RNA	A guest who is registered but not yet assigned a room
OOO	Blocked rooms in no specific location of the hotel
ROH	The room that has been paid for in advance (guaranteed)
slept-out	An extra charge for extra people occupying a room
DNA	A room that was thought to be occupied, but is available
overstays	A room that can't be occupied because of repairs being done
PIA	A double room with two double beds
OC	Did not arrive

CHAPTER PROJECTS

1. Draw a lobby floor plan for a 200-room, three-star hotel with a 50–50 percentage of leisure and business guests. Include the front desk with registration and cashier positions. Show the bellhop and concierge stations. Include seating areas. Describe or show samples and pictures of furnishings, floor coverings, fabrics, and other textures.

2. Pick two days next week and call a hotel and inquire about a reservation for that time. Ask for a standard double room. Inquire about AARP, AAA, corporate, and government rates for the same time frame.

3. List the events held in your area that might increase hotel room rates.

4. Call three properties to research their cancellation policies. Write about their differences.

5

FRONT-OFFICE OPERATIONS:
LUGGAGE, REGISTERING, ROOMING THE GUESTS, INFORMATION, MAIL, TELEPHONE

CHAPTER OUTLINE

LEARNING OBJECTIVES

After reading this chapter, you should be able to

- Trace the possible movements and placements of luggage during a guest's hotel stay.
- Discuss security from the standpoint of luggage, keys, and telephones.
- Describe mail handling procedures.
- Relate proper switchboard practices to be used in both small and large establishments.
- Complete registration forms and know methods of payment.

FIGURE 5-1

A hotel's bell staff transports luggage to guests' rooms. This time provides an excellent opportunity to "sell" the hotel.

After guests arrive, the front office is responsible for providing many services to ensure their satisfaction. In this chapter we will discuss registration, luggage handling, room keys, and rooming the guests. Providing information, receiving and delivering guests' mail, and administering telephone service are other services offered.

LUGGAGE HANDLING

Everyone who checks into a hotel has some kind of luggage. In large hotels it is up to the hotel personnel, specifically the bell staff, to move and carry this luggage to and from the guests' rooms.

In a large hotel the first person to greet a guest is the doorman. His duties include opening the car doors for the guests, opening and holding the hotel door for the guests, and signalling for a bellhop to take the luggage from the taxi or limousine and carry it inside the hotel. If the guests arrive in their own cars, the doorman calls for a bellhop,

signals a parking attendant to take the car to the garage, and gives the guests parking receipts.

Inside the hotel the luggage is placed in a central spot near the bell captain's desk while the guest is checking in. The bell staff has a system whereby the bellhops take turns carrying luggage. When the front desk signals a bellhop and gives him or her the room key, the luggage is carried or pushed on a cart to the room.

The arrival of large groups complicates luggage procedures. Large carts may be used if the rooms are blocked together; or the guests may carry their own luggage to their rooms.

The hotel/motel usually has a locked room adjacent to the lobby that is available to guests for holding their luggage. This is useful, for instance, when checkout time is 11 A.M. but the guest is not leaving the hotel until after lunch. The hotel is responsible for the luggage during this time and usually gives the guest a luggage check or receipt.

REGISTERING GUESTS

Anyone working in a hotel is a host or hostess. The guest's impressions are formed by all the workers in a hotel. The reservation clerk may have conveyed the first impression via phone, or the doorman might be the first personal contact with the hotel/motel. Often the desk clerk or room clerk presents the first impression for the guest.

A friendly smile is the number one requirement of the desk clerk. A pleasant greeting, such as "Good afternoon, sir, may I help you?" is given. The terms "sir," "ma'am," or "madam" should be used until the clerk learns the guest's name. Upon knowing the name, the clerk should use it immediately and frequently.

When registering a guest, the desk clerk locates the reservation card in the day's box or on the computer listing. If a room has not been assigned, the board or computer is checked for available rooms. Computerized hotels assign rooms from an up-to-the-minute status report which shows occupied and vacant rooms. It also indicates which ones are being cleaned or are out of service for repairs. See the computer printout showing room status in Figure 5-2.

Sometimes the desk clerk, using good personal judgment, might change the room assignment. The clerk is the person who actually sees the guest and can best judge which room would be most suitable. For example, a clerk might move an elderly couple to a ground-floor room. A clerk might also "sell up," persuading the guests that a higher priced room would better answer their needs.

ROOM TYPE	TOTAL	VACANT	OCCUPIED	DEPARTURES	ARRIVALS GTD	ARRIVALS N/G	OFF MARKET	AVAILABLE	PROJECTED % OCC.
					CURRENT BEDDED HOUSE STATUS 07/16/-- 09:30				
STND	120	53	63	30	31	14	4	35	66
KING	60	20	40	20	17	5		24	64
ESPC	4	1	3	1		2			100
HAND	4	1	3	1	1			1	76
EKTC	3	2	1					4	19
EPAR	1		1						100
EBDL	1	1						1	
KNSM	8	2	5			1	1	2	58
SNSM	10	5	5	1	3			5	57
ENSM	2	1	1	1				2	
TOTALS	213	86	122	54	52	22	5	74	

FIGURE 5-2

Room status computer printout

COMPLETING THE REGISTRATION CARD

After assigning the room the clerk gives the guest a *registration card* to fill out. This might be computer generated, requiring only the signature of the guest. The registration card acts as a contract between the guest and the hotel. These cards vary depending on the hotel, but they generally show the room number and ask for the information shown in the card in Figure 5-3. The card might indicate the method of payment, and, if applicable, the clerk can imprint or write the credit card number on the slip. The registration card may also show the number of people in a room and whether they are members of a group. Particularly at motor inns, automobile model, year, and license number are included on the registration card.

Often the registration card or computer form is multiple-copy. This enables the clerk to distribute copies to the bellhop, the telephone operators, and the accounting department.

Large groups may be preregistered. In these situations the members filled out registration cards prior to arrival and sent in guarantee payments. Preregistration is a time saver and eliminates standing in

NAME J.D. McHugh		
HOME ADDRESS 1319 Kings Highway Cincinnati, Ohio 45211		

NAME   J.D. McHugh

HOME ADDRESS   1319 Kings Highway
Cincinnati, Ohio 45211

COMPANY   Northern Graphics

COMPANY ADDRESS   100 Franklin Blvd.
Cincinnati, Oh 45202

MAKE OF CAR   Ford   LIC. NO. 000-AAA STATE OH

CREDIT CARD INFORMATION

☐ CASH   ☐ DIRECT CHARGE   ☐ CONTINENTAL EXPRESS

☐ CHECK   ☐ PLUS CREDIT CARD   ☐ UNITED CREDIT, INC

X   J.D. McHugh

I agree to be held personally liable for this bill should the indicated party fail to pay. I understand the hotel assumes no responsibility for damage or theft in parking areas or for valuables not secured at the front desk.

ROOM NUMBER 509   TYPE DBL-DBL RATE 92.00

DATE OF ARRIVAL 11/1/--   DATE OF DEPARTURE 11/2/--   GUARANTEED? Yes

NUMBER OF GUESTS 2   DEPOSIT 92.00   CREDIT CARD NUMBER D12345

RESERVED BY   J.D. McHugh

TELEPHONE   513-555-5574

CONF. NUMBER   A1084

☐ GSR

☐ GSM APPROVED

The
Wise Hotel

123 Berwinkle Boulevard
Los Angeles, California
90077-1024
1-213-555-2397

ROOM NUMBER 509   RATE 92.00

ARRIVAL 11/1/--   DEPARTURE 11/2/--

NUMBER OF GUESTS 2   DEPOSIT 92.00

NAME   J.D. McHugh

The
Wise Hotel

123 Berwinkle Boulevard
Los Angeles, California
90077-1024
1-213-555-2397

CHECK OUT TIME IS 11 AM

FIGURE 5-3

Registration card

lines. When conventions are held, the company or association may set up its own registration desk. The personnel working at this desk will take the room reservation cards and convey them to the front desk as well as handle the meeting registration. A tour group may also be routed to its own registration table. Rooming lists are used by the hotel/motel in these situations.

Dealing with Problems.   Problems naturally occur: A reservation card has disappeared or a room has not been blocked even though the guests insist they have a reservation. The solution to this type of problem can be easy. If there is space available, the clerk simply assigns a room without mentioning the problem to the guest.

If the hotel is fully booked, a complete investigation of records and reservations must be done with the cooperation of the reservation clerk and room clerk. Perhaps a date or name mix-up caused the problem and a room really is available. Or a sleeper might be discovered. If these alternatives fail, the guest might be offered, at a discount, a room that has a minor disrepair.

If no solution is found, the hotel should make all possible effort to *walk the guests,* by placing them in another hotel. This would involve a bellhop physically moving the guests and their luggage to the new location. Throughout this ordeal, the desk clerk must express regret. Offering the guest a free refreshment while other arrangements are being made is a thoughtful gesture and may help defuse angry feelings.

By all means, the details of the problem must be reported to the front-office manager to ensure that the situation will not occur again. Problem situations must be corrected as quickly as possible.

ISSUING ROOM KEYS

A hotel/motel usually gives out one key per guest room. If there is more than one guest in a room, a second key may be issued. The key could also be kept at the front desk on a rack, in the room's mail slot, or in a locked key cabinet or drawer beneath the front desk. A large hotel will have a key clerk whose duty involves handing out keys to the guests.

Great care must be taken for the security of the guests that the key is not given out incorrectly. Good judgment, discretion, and observation must be exercised by the key clerk or room clerk when releasing room keys.

In European hotels guests are expected to turn in their keys each time they leave the premises. The key is often on a key ring so large that no one would want to carry it. Some large European hotels have a person sitting at a table or desk on each floor who is in charge of room keys.

Innovations in the keying of rooms include guest-programmed combination locks and keys the size of plastic credit cards that fit into lock slots. The "punch card" or magnetic strip key system enables the front-desk clerk to repunch holes or reprogram a card for each room. These combination and plastic key lock systems provide ultimate security as they change with each new guest. The cards have no room number on them and usually not even the hotel name. They are given to the guest in a folder or envelope that displays that information.

The housekeeping department has access to all the room keys, punch cards, or master combinations. In addition, a master key is kept by the manager at the front desk. The security of the master key is extremely tight; only a few employees have access to it.

ROOMING THE GUESTS

In rooming the guests the desk clerk or room clerk presents the bellhop or the guest with the room key and a rooming slip. The *rooming slip* is usually a carbon copy of the registration card, but it may be a separate form the clerk fills out. This shows the guest's name, room number, and rate. A pleasant "Have a nice visit" or "We're happy to have you here" is then offered by the clerk.

FIGURE 5-4

Plastic key cards provide access to guest rooms.

The bellhop leads the way to the room, holding doors, and ringing for the elevator. While riding the elevator, the bellhop should engage the guest in pleasant conversation, "selling" all the while. For instance, this would be an appropriate time to mention the hotel's fine restaurants.

The bellhop unlocks and inspects the room to be sure all is in order. The heating and air conditioning systems are explained, lights turned on, and curtains opened. The guest is given the key with a pleasant "Let me know if I can be of further service." If offered, the tip is accepted graciously and discreetly.

PROVIDING INFORMATION

There are two types of information that the front desk will be asked to provide: information about the hotel's operations and general information. Often in-room televisions provide information about hotel activities and area tourist attractions. Printed matter in the room also provides such information.

INFORMATION ABOUT THE HOTEL

The front-desk clerks will be asked such questions about the hotel's operations as:

What time does the restaurant open for dinner? Where is the National Association of Pipe Fitters Meeting? When is checkout time?

In convention hotels the most common questions concern the meeting room a group's sessions are being held in. This information should be on a board such as shown in Figure 5-5. All employees in the front office or lobby must be able to answer these types of questions. Information given on hotel activities must be accurate. Each day the front-desk employees should review the hotel services, activities, and events for that day.

GENERAL INFORMATION

The second kind of information that is needed is more general:

Is there a gym nearby? What time do stores close? What sight-seeing tours can I take around here? Where is a nearby Catholic Church?

Large hotels/motels will have a specific information desk staffed throughout the day to answer these types of questions. The person manning the information desk may have the title "concierge." This person should be thoroughly familiar with the city. Brochures from local tourist attractions, tour companies, and listings of current events should be available from the concierge. Local maps, telephone books, entertainment guides, and transportation time tables make up the information desk's library. The concierge may be called upon to procure tickets for cultural or recreational activities. The concierge sometimes acts as travel agent, changing or making transportation reservations for guests.

A guest may also ask the front-desk clerk to personally recommend a restaurant. If the hotel has a restaurant, of course the clerk would recommend it. Otherwise, or if pushed for a local restaurant, the clerk can give his or her personal opinion. However, it is wise to consult a co-worker, both for giving the guest a suggestion or confirming a suggestion.

General information should be as accurate as possible. Reference books on the local area should also be available to the front-desk staff. If an employee can't answer a question, the guest should be referred to the local newspaper or entertainment guide. City magazines or

FIGURE 5-5

Daily events roster

tour guides might be placed in each room. Some large hotels offer printed schedules of events taking place within the hotel. An example of this is shown in Figure 5-6.

HANDLING GUESTS' MAIL

Very little guest mail is received by hotels today because of the use of fax machines and e-mail. However, great care must be given to handling guests' mail since the loss of an important letter on the part of the hotel could result in a lawsuit against the establishment. A log or record is kept of all incoming mail. This provides proof of how the hotel handled the mail and enables the hotel to trace lost mail.

Many hotels have a ***time stamp*** and stamp each item as it is received. In traditional properties, letter mail is then placed in the mail or key rack in the numbered slot. The rack is arranged vertically by floor and horizontally by room number and can easily be seen by the guests. The mail slots are checked each day by the room clerks or someone designated as mail clerk. In a large hotel a mail clerk might be a specific position. If it is observed that a letter has

Gateway Events

Lounge Activities

Visit the Blackjack table in the Silver Slipper Lounge for some Las Vegas-style gambling. The stakes here are fun and entertainment, not money. Test your skill. Monday - Saturday 5:00 p.m. - 2:00 a.m.

Happy Hour - A complimentary buffet Monday - Friday from 4:00 p.m. - 7:00 p.m. in the Silver Slipper Lounge.

Gateway Bar - Let Karen Rose entertain you at the Piano Bar. Wednesday through Saturday 8:00 p.m. - Midnight.

Restaurants

Try the new menu in the Golden Coin Restaurant. The features are tender steaks and fresh seafood. Also two daily specials each evening.

The Colonial Restaurant features Midwestern cuisine at its finest. The menus change weekly and specials are offered on a daily basis.

Sunday brunch is offered every week in the Gateway Bar from 8:30 a.m. - 2:00 p.m.

Recreation

Swimming pools/Sauna - Our indoor pool is located on the 7th floor and is open all year. The outdoor pool is located in a garden setting and is open from Memorial Day to Labor Day, 10:00 a.m. - 10:00 p.m. The Sauna, open from 7:00 a.m. to 10:00 p.m. daily, will ease all your tensions after a hectic day of business or sightseeing. The sauna is located on the 7th floor near the indoor pool.

Golf - Try out our 18-hole championship golf course. Our golf professional Barbara Palmer and her staff will assist in any way they can to help you enjoy your game.

Tennis - Our three lighted tennis courts are located by the garden and outdoor pool.

Gateway Resort

FIGURE 5-6

Schedule of hotel events

FIGURE 5-7

Hotels put a time stamp on mail as it is received, then place it in guests' mail slots.

not been picked up, a bellhop might be sent to deliver it to the guest's room.

Packages received from the Postal Service, FedEx, UPS, and other courier services are time stamped as well. The mail clerk or bell captain also makes out a receipt which the guest must sign to receive the package. This is also true of insured, registered, or special-delivery letters. The bellhop usually takes special-delivery mail or packages directly to the room and gets the guest's signature on the receipt. The hotel might place a bulky package in the luggage or package room and signal the guest of its arrival with a note in his or her mailbox. Conference materials constitute a large percentage of mail.

Many hotels have small lights connected to the telephone system that can be lit to let the guest know there is a message or piece of mail waiting. When the mail is received by the hotel, the mail clerk or desk clerk would notify the hotel telephone operator. The operator would turn on the light on the guest's room phone and inform the guest of the mail when he or she calls. Notification of mail can be entered into the computer under the guest's name. Sophisticated in-room interactive televisions that provide guests information whenever the set is turned on can furnish mail notification. Electronic checkout and plastic key cards make it possible for a guest to check in the hotel and never be in contact with the front

desk again. Under such circumstances it is the guest's responsibility to inquire for letter-mail or packages. The front desk and/or bell captain should keep a list of guests who have asked about expected mail.

COD (cash on delivery) packages must be processed through the accounting department and cashier. It depends on hotel policy whether or not these are accepted. If the charge is paid by the hotel, it is entered on the guest's account.

The hotel forwards mail to the guest's home address for a limited time after the guest departs. If a letter is special delivery or registered, the hotel returns it to the delivery service for handling.

ADMINISTERING TELEPHONE SERVICE

The *switchboard,* or central telephone mechanism, is a vital part of the smooth operations of hospitality establishments. It processes both incoming and outgoing calls and is a very influential factor in guests' satisfaction.

When a guest checks in, a portion of the registration slip denoting the room number is immediately given to the switchboard, or the room number is conveyed to the phone system through the computer. When the guest checks out, automatically the information is conveyed immediately to the operator.

In a large hotel/motel establishment the switchboard or PBX system may be very complicated. Often there are several operators working eight-hour shifts around the clock. Sophisticated electronic phone systems require very little bookkeeping; the charges for any calls made from a guest's room are posted automatically to the guest's folio.

In many properties there is a charge even for local calls. This can range from 50 cents to over $1.00. Long-distance calls may have a surcharge placed on them above normal rates. In some countries abroad, hotel long-distance charges are so high that travelers use public telephones or ask for an immediate call-back from the people they are phoning. Some properties add fees for 1-800/888, credit card, and collect calls. One of the amenities that some properties advertise is "free local phone calls," and no-charge for 1-800/888 and credit card calls can also be a promotional tool.

Most rooms have phones with the dial or push buttons coded, for example, "2" for Room Service, "8" for outside calls, and "9" for long distance. In a smaller motel or inn, the communications system is of-

ten handled by a lone front-desk clerk. The rooms in these smaller facilities might have phones with no dials. If the guest picks the phone up to make a call, the front desk answers and connects the call. The charge would be manually written on the guest's account.

More and more guests are using their cell phones from hotel rooms. Many electronic rooms of today have modems for computer and fax connections. E-mail communications is commonplace in many properties.

PHONE SECURITY

In most hotels policy prohibits operators from giving out room numbers of guests. This protects their privacy and prevents thievery. If a caller asks for a room number, the operator does not give out that information but replies "May I ring the room for you?" The operator has an alphabetical listing by last names of all guests from the registration form. Usually these are automated and appear rapidly on a computer screen.

The same is true when a lobby phone is used. The lobby phone is connected directly to the switchboard where operators take the calls. If front-desk personnel are asked for a room number by a lobby visitor, they would direct the person to the lobby phone. If someone picks up the lobby phone and asks "What room is John Jones in?" the operator replies, "I'll connect you to Mr. Jones' room." The room number is not given out by either front-desk clerks or the hotel operator.

MESSAGES

Voice mail or its equivalent has lessened the responsibility of conveying messages. Yet messages may be taken for guests on a standard message form in smaller properties as shown in Figure 5-8. The form is given to the desk clerk or the key clerk to be placed in the mail or key rack. Usually a carbon copy of the message is kept by the operator for the hotel's records. As was discussed under notification of mail, interactive televisions can act as phone message centers for guests. More and more properties are using in-room voice mail for guests. This obviously reduces the responsibility of the switchboard. When a guest checks in, any messages already taken may be attached to the registration card or signaled in the computer reservation and presented to the guest by the desk clerk. When the hotel operators are notified of an arrival, they immediately give any

---

TELEPHONE MESSAGE

Date _____ Time _____

To _____ Room _____

From _____

_____

Will call again _____ Please return call _____

Message _____

_____

_____

Operator _____

THE BIG APPLE
HOTEL

FIGURE 5-8

Telephone message form

messages that had been set aside to the incoming guest, or those that have been keyed in the computer to print out with the registration form.

Most meeting rooms include in-house telephones that accommodate inter-hotel and incoming calls. The meeting coordinator decides where the phone line will be installed, within the meeting room or outside at its entrance. Calls to individual meeting attendees are forwarded to that line. The hotel operator is instructed about which calls to forward to that phone. Meeting officials usually take and convey messages, often on a bulletin board upon which call memos are pinned, folded in half so that the recipients see only their name and no one else can see the message. If the meeting has a "no calls" policy, the meeting coordinator is asked to report to the front desk or switchboard periodically to pick up all the messages that have been received.

TYPES OF CALLS

The switchboard handles four types of calls:

1. Outside calls coming into the hotel, both for guests and for employees.
2. Guests calling other rooms or departments inside the hotel if they cannot dial direct.
3. Calls from public rooms within the hotel.
4. Employees calling other departments within the hotel. Often a "beeper" system is used to supplement these calls.

Outside calls should take priority and be answered first with a cheerful "Good Morning, Wise Hotel," for example. Next in priority would be answering calls from guest rooms, with "Hotel operator, may I help you?" Calls from public rooms, such as the lobby or a meeting room, would be answered next with the same greeting. Calls from employee lines would be answered last.

Incoming calls are answered on a first-come, first-served basis. If two lines ring almost simultaneously, the second is answered and asked "Would you hold, please?" or told "One moment, please," and the first is then answered and directed. If talking to one line when another rings, the operator would ask the party to hold a moment; the operator would then answer the incoming call with, "One moment please," and return to the original caller.

Wake-up calls are standard in most lodging establishments. Be warned that a hotel can be sued for the losses suffered by a guest who was not awakened at the time requested. A guest could miss a vital appointment or an airline flight if not awakened.

Wake-up calls can be generated by a computer. When the guest calls, the operator keys in the correct call time and the room is automatically rung at the requested time. With voice recognition technology, a total computer system may be in operation. The guest calls and gets recorded prompts to press the desired wake-up time into the phone-pad, followed by a number to signify A.M. or P.M. For example, "2" may indicate A.M. and "7," P.M. An early morning call might involve pressing 6452, for 6:45 A.M.

In noncomputerized properties, the operator keeps a wake-up call sheet as shown in Figure 5-9.

When receiving a wake-up call request, the operator should always repeat the time to the guest to be perfectly sure that the correct time slot has been marked. For personal wake-up at the appropriate time, the operator calls the room and says "Good morning, it's seven

Date	April 15, 20— —							THE BIG APPLE HOTEL				
Room	Time	6:00	6:15	6:30	6:45	7:00	7:15	7:30	7:45	8:00	8:15
#401	8:00									401	
#402	7:30							402			
#403	6:30			403							
#404	7:00					404					
#405	7:15						405				

FIGURE 5-9

Wake-up call sheet

o'clock." If there is no answer, the operator should call back every five minutes for at least half an hour. Many rooms have clock radios giving guests another wake-up option.

In-house calls from room to room or from room to restaurant are not charged. Charges for local calls and long-distance calls are tallied on the guest's bill.

Long-distance call policy in hotels varies. Some hotels will accept collect calls. The long-distance operator says, "Collect call for Mr. Jones," and the hotel operator calls Mr. Jones' room to inquire if he will accept the charges. In the past, the telephone company operator was asked to give *time and charges* so the call could be properly billed. When the call was completed, the long-distance operator rang back and quoted the charges for the call. This was written on a voucher and given to the front-desk clerk or given directly to the accounting department. Most telephone systems in hotels have the capability of automatically posting charges when a guest makes a long-distance call from the room. Computers are interfaced with the telephone system and long-distance charges are almost instantaneously posted on the guest's folio.

SWITCHBOARD OPERATORS

There are several prerequisites for switchboard operators. They must have pleasant, understandable voices. They should be very courteous

as they are often the first contact a person has with the establishment. "Thank you" should be said with each request. "Will you hold please?" is the proper response when a line is busy. When the line is available, "I can connect you now, sir/madam. Thank you for holding" is an appropriate reply.

Operators must be speedy and accurate. No one likes to hold or listen to a ringing tone. Operators must avoid wasting time by gaining complete information about the nature of the call. Tact must be used in graciously trying to find out the reason for incoming calls. For example, when someone asks for the manager, the operator might ask, "Are you calling about a conference schedule?" and steer the party toward the sales office. In essence, the switchboard operator is a salesperson, time manager, psychologist, and diplomat.

TRENDS

Adaptations of credit cards and the advent of *smart cards* will diminish the use of room keys as we know them now. A smart card looks like a plastic credit card but contains incredible amounts of information about the holder. Magnetic strips on smart cards can give not only credit information, but health data and complete personal identification. The front desk will be able to program the smart card, via radio, to allow a guest access to the room. The access is erased upon checkout. Housekeeping employees will have cards programmed to allow them entrance to rooms for cleaning. Security is further advanced by illegal room access being immediately radioed to the guard station.

In-room television information will cut down somewhat on the need of information specialists in the lobby area. Still, people will have queries and requests while in the lobby and also a need to communicate with a person. As the individual use of personal telephone systems grows, the workload of switchboard operators will lessen.

CHAPTER ACTIVITIES

FRONT-OFFICE OPERATIONS: LUGGAGE, REGISTERING, ROOMING THE GUESTS, INFORMATION, MAIL, TELEPHONE

1. Fill out the registration card for the following persons:

Mr. & Mrs. James Doyle, 2278 Carrie Lane, Atlanta, GA 30345, Ford, license GA ABC-123, Phone: 404-555-0938, ARR 8/8 DEP 8/10, Double at $52/United Credit #123-456-79

NAME	ROOM NUMBER TYPE RATE	ROOM NUMBER RATE
HOME ADDRESS	DATE OF ARRIVAL DATE OF DEPARTURE GUARANTEED?	ARRIVAL DEPARTURE
COMPANY		
COMPANY ADDRESS	NUMBER OF GUESTS DEPOSIT CREDIT CARD NUMBER	NUMBER OF GUESTS DEPOSIT
MAKE OF CAR LIC. NO. STATE	RESERVED BY TELEPHONE	NAME
CREDIT CARD INFORMATION ☐ CASH ☐ DIRECT CHARGE ☐ CONTINENTAL EXPRESS ☐ CHECK ☐ PLUS CREDIT CARD ☐ LIMITED CREDIT, INC	CONF. NUMBER	
X _____	☐ GSR	
I agree to be held personally liable for this bill should the indicated party fail to pay. I understand the hotel assumes no responsibility for damage or theft in parking areas or for valuables not secured at the front desk.	☐ GSM APPROVED The Wise Hotel	The Wise Hotel

2. Fill out the phone message below using the following information:

   Betty Dorsey called this morning at 10:00 to speak with Larry Harris, director of sales. Her phone number is 555-1234.

TELEPHONE MESSAGE

Date _____ Time _____

To _____ Room _____

From _____

_____

Will call again _____ Please return call _____

Message _____

_____

_____

Operator _____

THE BIG APPLE
HOTEL

---

3. List the reference items from your area that you feel a local hotel's information desk should keep on hand to answer general information questions.

4. Make a list of all the possible hotel amenities and benefits that a bellhop might discuss while rooming the guest.

CHAPTER PROJECTS

1. Write a short play about a guest arriving and his or her reservation being lost and there being no available room. Act out with another student playing desk clerk what ensues.

2. Shadow a hotel switchboard operator for two hours and record the number of calls received by type:

   Outside coming in
   Guests calling within the hotel
   Calls from public rooms
   Interdepartmental calls

3. Poll your local hotel/motels concerning the security measures they take handling room keys.

FRONT-OFFICE OPERATIONS:
ACCOUNTING AND CHECKING OUT

CHAPTER OUTLINE

LEARNING OBJECTIVES

After reading this chapter, you should be able to

- Manually complete folios.
- Describe methods of payment and the precautions taken with each.
- Explain the night auditor's duties.
- List the functions of a hotel cashier.
- Trace the activities that take place during checkout.

ACCOUNTING

Guests pay for the hospitality services that they receive at a lodging establishment when they check out. The management of collecting money from guests is vital. Payments from guests are collected by front-desk clerks, or specific cashier positions may be established. Any personnel involved in collecting payments from guests must have been trained to be discreet and amiable. The accounting department, which is also called the "back office," works closely with the front-desk personnel. This division is responsible for billings and accounts payable, financial statements, payroll, profit and loss statements, and yield management statistics.

DETERMINING THE BILL

How is the total bill for a guest determined? Basically, there is a set room rate (rack rate) that was established when the guest checked in. This is quoted on the registration card. To this a sales tax and, in many localities, a higher lodging tax are added. Lodging taxes can add considerably to a person's bill. In addition to standard state and local sales taxes, some areas add a flat rate "bed tax" on each night's lodging. In some cities these add up to 17 percent of the total room cost. These funds may be used to support tourism promotion or building projects. For example, Houston's high lodging taxes are used to finance the construction of the Astrodome. Figure 6-1 shows combined bed, state, and local taxes by U.S. regions.

In addition, the guest has most likely incurred charges for using the telephone. The guest may have charged meals and drinks in the restaurant and bar, or there may be a charge for food that room service delivered to the room. In a large hotel the guest might have charged to the room flowers from the florist or toothpaste from the gift shop. All of these additional charges must be tallied for the guest at checkout time. Long-term guests at extended-stay properties may pay weekly, or their bills are invoiced directly to their company. This may involve a purchase order from the company.

Folios.   A *folio* is kept for each guest. This is a running tabulation of the charges a guest has incurred from all the departments of the hotel. The folio keeps accounts that are due and those that are paid. Computerized folio systems can show folios on the screen and print them out at the touch of a button.

The sample computer folio in Figure 6-2 shows that upon arrival the guest paid $46.00 for her room and $5.06 tax. The next day she

Averaged bed, state, and local taxes in state markets

Northeast	Percent	South Central	Percent
Connecticut	12.00	Arkansas	10.63
Maine	7.00	Kentucky	11.83
Massachusetts	12.45	Louisiana	11.02
New Hampshire	8.00	Mississippi	9.94
New York	14.30	Oklahoma	10.39
Rhode Island	12.00	Texas	15.00
Vermont	9.00	**North Central**	
Mid-Atlantic		Iowa	12.00
Delaware	8.00	Kansas	11.15
Maryland	12.50	Missouri	13.29
New Jersey	9.44	Nebraska	14.84
Pennsylvania	12.33	North Dakota	9.00
(District of Columbia)	15.60	South Dakota	9.00
Great Lakes States		**Northwest**	
Illinois	14.90	Idaho	11.00
Indiana	11.00	Montana	4.00
Michigan	15.00	Oregon	9.00
Minnesota	12.25	Washington	12.05
Ohio	13.58	Wyoming	8.00
Wisconsin	11.76	**Southwest**	
Southeast		Arizona	10.63
Alabama	10.00	California	12.00
Florida	11.50	Colorado	11.80
Georgia	14.00	Nevada	9.00
North Carolina	12.00	New Mexico	10.62
South Carolina	12.00	Utah	10.60
Tennessee	12.91	Hawaii	10.16
Virginia	11.50	Alaska	8.00
West Virginia	9.00		

Occupancy taxes vary in local jurisdictions. Percentages reflect averaged taxes for some states with diverse markets.

FIGURE 6-1

Combined tax amounts vary in local jurisdictions. Percentages reflect averaged taxes for some states with diverse markets.
Source: American Hotel Foundation

paid another $51.06 for the lodging but wound up with a balance of only $47.93 when she made a long-distance call which cost $3.13. The next morning before checking out she made two more calls which left her owing the hotel $9.48.

```
ROOM #:      1207/  5              Regist Num. 27584    Clk 6       Folio 1
Name            SPENCER, Deanna    Days 2
Type of Pay   CASH                 Rate  $ 46.00
Description                        Postings  9


CLERK #    DATE       DEPARTMENT      AMOUNT    BALANCE    DESCRIPTION

2653    SEP 03 --    CASH PAYMENTS   $51.06    $51.06     UPON ARRIVAL
   9    SEP 03 --    ROOM            $46.00    $ 5.06     RM #1207 RATE 46
   9    SEP 03 --    TAX             $ 5.06    $ 0.00
9503    SEP 04 --    CASH PAYMENT    $51.06    $51.06     2ND NIGHT PAYMENT
9403    SEP 04 --    LONG DISTANCE   $ 3.13    $47.93     501-555-7645
   9    SEP 04 --    ROOM            $46.00    $ 1.93     RM #1207 RATE 46
   9    SEP 04 --    TAX             $ 5.06    $ 3.13
8503    SEP 05 --    LONG DISTANCE   $ 0.62    $ 3.75     501-555-1212
8403    SEP 05 -     LONG DISTANCE   $ 5.73    $ 9.48     501-555-7645


                    THIS is NOT a BILL.
                    Advance copy for your Review
```

FIGURE 6-2

Computer folio

Handwritten folios are still occasionally used in smaller hotels. Understanding them makes computer usage simpler. Handwritten (or manual) folios, in multiple copies, are kept in a *bucket* (usually a metal oblong portable box) at the front desk near the cashier's pen.

A manual folio might have seven columns for the seven days of the week and, along the side, a list of the departments most often used by guests. Charges are posted by day across from the appropriate department. Each day each department's charges are inserted. Balances from day to day are totaled by the night auditor. A sample form for a handwritten folio is shown in Figure 6-3.

Vouchers.   In noncomputerized properties, when the hotel telephone operator or the restaurant cashier receives a charge to the guest, that person sends a *voucher* to the front desk which shows the amount of the charge. Vouchers are forwarded to the front desk as quickly as possible after charges are incurred, as guests can check out at any time. The voucher is time stamped upon receipt at the front desk. The clerk then posts the amount on the guest's folio and initials the voucher to show that it has been posted. The folio is then

Room No. 206	No. Persons 2	Rate $92	Arrival 6/5/--	Departure 6/7/--	No. 51113

NAME: Mr. and Mrs. John McGrath

The Wise Hotel

SIGNATURE: John McGrath

Old Folio No.   51112

Next Folio No.   51114

DATE	6/5	6/6	6/7				
Balance Forward							
Room	$92.00	$92.00					
Tax	5.06	5.06					
Telephone (LOCAL)	1.08	4.80					
Telephone (L.D.)	12.40						
Laundry							
Food	60.64	23.82	18.44				
Beverages		12.54					
Cash Disbursements							
Transfer							
TOTAL	171.18	138.22	18.44				
Cash Receipts	—	—	327.84				
Transfer							
Allowances							
BALANCE			—				

FIGURE 6-3

Handwritten folio

returned to the bucket, and the vouchers are kept filed by date and department.

With computerized systems, posting is done at the ***point of sale (POS).*** For example, a meal is charged and the cashier in the restaurant keys in the total at his or her terminal. This total is instantaneously included on the folio when it is called up on any terminal in the hotel.

Credits.   Credits also are recorded on the folio. Credits might occur for several reasons. A guest might pay a portion of the bill. The cashier

then credits the guests' folio with a payment. If one guest pays for another, both folios need to be updated. For one a charge would be added; for the other a credit would be entered.

There might also be an adjustment, rebate, or allowance added to the guest's bill. For example, a customer might be given credit for a telephone call that was incorrectly charged to that room. Each facility has different policies concerning this, but usually the manager must approve such adjustments. When approved, a **rebate voucher** is prepared and the amount is posted as a credit to the guest's folio. A rebate journal is also kept so that the night auditor can justify and cross-check these folio entries.

COLLECTING PAYMENT

A hotel must establish very early that a guest will be able to pay the bill. The lodging industry is a service industry, and services already rendered cannot be repossessed. Many hotels, particularly those along interstate highways in highly transient locations, require that a person pay for the room in advance. To ensure payment of all additional charges, the motel might charge a deposit for the room key. When the guest returns the key to collect the deposit, the hotel checks to see if additional charges such as long-distance telephone calls have been entered on the folio. A common last-minute addition to a bill is charges for items consumed from in-room minibars. Most often this involves an employee making a physical check of its inventory.

METHODS OF PAYMENT

Guests may use cash, checks, charges, credit cards, or vouchers in paying their hotel bills. Each of these methods is discussed in the following sections. Acceptable methods of payment should be clearly stated to the guest at check-in. Often this is printed on the rooming slip or key folder. If a property doesn't take personal checks, or specific brand credit cards, guests deserve to know this before incurring charges.

Cash.   Some guests present cash and should be given a receipt. The cashier should post the transaction immediately on the folio. The cashier posts these transactions on the front-office cash sheet, which records in chronological order all the cash received and all that has been disbursed from that office.

The cashier has begun the day with a *bank,* which is a set amount of cash in the register. During the day checks may be cashed and these must tally with the amount of cash left in the bank. The cash sheet must be justified at the end of the day with the paid out vouchers. *Paid outs* might be for COD deliveries or tips. If, for example, a guest signs for room service and adds a tip for the bellhop, then the bellhop can go to the cashier and immediately receive the tip amount. A paid out voucher would be written up. If the hotel has a computerized system, the cashier's terminal can access and print out guest folios. A computer can also keep track of paid outs and reconcile them with the bank amount.

Particularly in big cities, large hotels develop policies concerning cashiers accepting foreign currency. Foreign currency must be converted into U.S. dollars, so an arrangement with a bank or foreign money broker must be established. Even for the more stable currencies, like German marks or French francs, rates fluctuate daily, so cashiers must communicate with the accepting banks as to the current rate of exchange.

Checks.   House policies vary, but cashiers must take a few standard precautions for accepting checks. The cashier must (1) be sure the check is not postdated; (2) be sure the amount is correct; and (3) be sure the signature is signed in his or her presence. On the back of the check the cashier should note some other means of identification, usually a driver's license and a major credit card number. Most hotels do not accept third-party checks.

Most establishments will cash recognized money orders and traveler's checks. Both must be countersigned in the presence of the cashier, who must make sure that the signatures match. Identification such as a driver's license or a passport is usually requested.

Charges.   A line of credit can be established either for the guest or for the guest's company. In these instances the hotel would send a bill to the person or business at a later date. A credit account would be carefully checked, most likely with the guest's personal or company bank. There are varying accounts or lines of credit that a person can charge. This could be as low as $50, but at some hotels a $500 line of credit would mean only two night's lodging. Hotel policies on "credit line" accounts vary, with the manager having the final approval or disapproval. Direct billing is most often used at extended-stay properties for their long-term guests.

Credit Cards.   Upon registering, hotels ask the guest how the bill will be paid. If it is a credit card, the number is checked against the

credit card company information which shows expired and stolen cards and bad risk holders. In many instances, when guests make reservations they guarantee it by giving their credit card number. The guest may prefer to pay in cash upon checkout, but if not the hotel by that time has had the opportunity to establish the guest's credit-worthiness.

Most places that accept credit cards are connected electronically with "swipe" equipment connected to the issuing bank. This automatically authorizes that a card is valid, that the account is not in arrears, and that the credit limit is available. An authorization number is sometimes given. The credit limit or *floor limit* imposed on the individual's account is very important with today's high room rates. For example, a guest may have a $3,000 credit limit. When the hotel checks the authorization service, it learns that $2,500 has already been used. If the hotel allows the guest to charge over $500, the credit card company might not accept the charges.

Different establishments honor different credit cards. Bank credit cards are the most common, usually Visa or Master Card. There are also travel and entertainment cards such as American Express and Diner's Club. With bank cards, the owed funds are quickly deposited in the hotel's account. Entertainment cards process payments periodically. In all cases, the hotel pays a commission to the credit companies on the charges made. This varies between 1 and 6 percent on the charged transaction. The hotel is billed the amount owed to the credit card company on a regular basis. In accepting a credit card, the cashier must be sure the card has been checked against the company's poor risk list and credit limit is available. The cashier should compare signatures on the card itself with the charge slip. The guest should be given a copy of the charge slip and folio showing a zero balance.

Prepaid Vouchers. A package tour might involve airfare to Jamaica, airport transfers, and three nights' lodging at a resort. In this case, the tour operator books and pays for the room nights for the traveler. The traveler presents vouchers that were given to him or her by the tour operator to the front desk. These indicate that the room nights have been paid. This also can occur with conference attendees. Vouchers are also used in the case of gift certificates or frequent-user awards.

THE CITY LEDGER

When guests check out, their folio is closed. In most cases the bill is paid in full, leaving a zero balance. Even if there is a balance when the

FIGURE 6-4

Different establishments honor different credit cards.

guest leaves, the folio is closed, and the amount due is transferred to what is called the city ledger. The *city ledger* shows all of the money owed to the hotel/motel.

Credit card billings are posted on the city ledger, showing that the credit card company has not paid that bill yet. Some companies and organizations have direct billing on a monthly basis. These bills are also included on the city ledger. Individuals or organizations that hold meetings at the property might also be direct billed. *Skippers* or *walk-outs* (guests who have left without paying their room charge), late charges (long-distance phone charges which were not picked up on the folio or computer prior to when the guest checked out), disputed bills, and bad checks all are included on the city ledger.

FIGURE 6-5

The night auditor gathers important statistics for management and also for the sales department.

THE NIGHT AUDITOR

The *night auditor* or auditors begin work after most of the hotel's departments have closed for the day. Auditors usually work from 11 P.M. to 7 A.M. An auditor finalizes the accounting for the hotel for the day and also compiles valuable research statistics for the property. The auditor position is generally not entry level, and often a cashier or room clerk is promoted to this slot.

The auditor pulls each individual guest folio up on the computer or manually retrieves the folios from the bucket, and inserts the room rate and taxes for that night. The room rate is verified. Credit limits are reviewed to be sure that the guest is not nearing his or her limit. The housekeeping department records are reviewed to ensure that there are no sleepers.

All point of sale debits and credits for the day are totaled and this is compared with the guests' folios to be sure all charges have been correctly entered. Charges for meeting rooms are posted. The auditor tallies each department's fiscal balance and confirms cash sheets and banks, recording overages and underages. Most importantly, the auditor updates the city ledger.

The auditor gathers important statistics for management and the sales department. The statistics answer the following questions management must know to run an efficient operation: Did all of those with reservations arrive? How many **walk-ins** (people with no reservations who appear at a property desiring a room) were there? What was the number of **no-shows** (people with reservations who don't come to the hotel)? Were there any skippers? What was the percentage of **overstays** and **understays** (guests who do not stay at the hotel for the entire time originally indicated)? Were the rates charged over or under the rack rate?

This information, along with variables such as the weather, time of year, airline schedules, and seasonal events, allows management to estimate the occupancy rate and to make projections. By the time the general manager arrives the next morning, the auditor has prepared a full report on the revenue generated the prior day and the statistical information needed to figure productivity and to make long-range plans for effective yield management.

The computer printout shown in Figure 6-6 is a departmental report showing debits and credits for the different hotel accounts and departments. The income from restaurants and bars is shown, and charges for long-distance calls and even the parking fees are shown. The night auditor compares these credits and debits with cash received, vouchers, and charges to folios.

Property management systems (PMSs) are computer programs that perform much of the tedious night auditor's accounting duties. Though the computer inserts the figures, a detail-oriented person must organize the data.

CHECKING OUT THE GUEST

Lodging facilities usually have a standard checkout time for all guests. After that time a guest must pay an additional day's rental. The standard checkout time most often is 11 A.M. A late checkout is sometimes requested by a guest. The last session of a conference might be a luncheon meeting at noon. A flight might not leave until late afternoon. The front

```
                              Department Report

     15705
                                            Midwestern Inns
     DATE        0905--           TIME   1:17:52 p.m.


     DEPARTMENT AND CORRECTION TOTALS for terminal :
     ***********************************************************************
     DEPARTMENT          CORRECT TOTALS          DAILY TOTALS          NET TOTALS
     ***********************************************************************
     ROOM                0  $    0.00        0  $    0.00        $    0.00
     TAX                 0  $    0.00        0  $    0.00        $    0.00
     LONG DISTANCE       0  $    0.00        4  $   14.44        $   14.44
     LOCAL PHONE         0  $    0.00        0  $    0.00        $    0.00
     LAUNDRY             0  $    0.00        0  $    0.00        $    0.00
     PARKING             0  $    0.00        1  $    4.00        $    4.00
     MISCELLANEOUS       1  $-  68.82        2  $   68.82        $    0.00
     GATEWAY BAR         1  $-   3.68        7  $   70.73        $   67.05
     BANQUET             0  $    0.00        0  $    0.00        $    0.00
     PAID OUT            0  $    0.00        0  $    0.00        $    0.00
     GRATUITY            0  $    0.00        0  $    0.00        $    0.00
     ROOM SERVICE        0  $    0.00        0  $    0.00        $    0.00
     COVER CHARGE        0  $    0.00        0  $    0.00        $    0.00
     ADMISSION TX        0  $    0.00        0  $    0.00        $    0.00

     DEBIT TOTALS        2  $-  72.50       14  $  157.99        $   85.49

     TRANS DEBIT         0  $    0.00        3  $  368.66        $  368.66
     C/C TRANSFER        0  $    0.00       11  $ 1101.38        $ 1101.38
     TRANS CREDIT        0  $    0.00        4  $- 688.34        $- 688.34
     CREDIT CARD         0  $    0.00       11  $-1101.38        $-1101.38
     CASH PAYMENT        0  $    0.00        3  $- 294.41        $- 294.41
     PAID CHECK          0  $    0.00        0  $    0.00        $    0.00
     ADJUSTMENT          0  $    0.00        0  $    0.00        $    0.00
     C/C DISCOUNT        0  $    0.00        0  $    0.00        $    0.00
     CORRECTION          0  $    0.00        0  $    0.00        $    0.00

     CRED. TOTALS        0  $    0.00       32  $- 614.09        $- 614.09


     NET DIFFE           2  $-  72.50        0  $- 456.10        $- 528.60
```

FIGURE 6-6

Departmental Accounting Report

desk in coordination with the housekeeping department determines if the late checkout is feasible without jeopardizing daily room sales. The hotel should offer luggage storage if needed by guests who must check out of their room, but are not yet departing. Hospitality rooms with comfortable seating and a T.V. can be set up for circumstances mentioned.

In a large hotel where in-person checkout is required, the set checkout time makes for quite a crowd at the cashier's cage and the front desk. Checking out a guest involves many people, and this last impression is most important. Selling a good impression of the hotel is still an aim, even though the guest is leaving.

NOTIFYING THE FRONT DESK

In fully computerized properties, a guest does not have to approach the front desk or cashier to check out. With T.V. in-room interface, a guest can tune to a channel that shows the complete folio or bill. The guest is instructed what action to take to approve the bill for payment. Room keys are left in the room or placed in a key box in the lobby upon departure. Checkout T.V. terminals may be placed in the lobby if guest rooms are not interfaced with such a system.

The checkout procedure in noncomputerized properties is more complicated. Sometimes guests will give notice that they are checking out by calling and asking for the front desk or the cashier. The hotel telephone operator should ask if the guest is checking out and explain, particularly in a computerized property, that the bill is ready. This saves the front-desk employees time. The operator should then ask if the guest needs a bellhop sent up to the room. If the guest says that he or she does need a bellhop, the operator would notify the bell captain. A bellhop goes to the room and then quickly looks around the room to be sure nothing is being left. While escorting the guests to the front desk, the bellhop carries on polite conversation and inquires about transportation needs. He notifies the doorman if a taxi is needed.

CASHIER'S CHECKOUT PROCEDURES

Large hotels may have a dozen personnel with the duties of cashier. A small establishment might have the desk clerk doubling as cashier. No matter who performs this function, the cashier should give a good last impression of the hotel. The cashier has the final opportunity to convince guests to return or to motivate them to tell friends about the establishment—the final selling time.

The cashier must give prompt attention to guests waiting to pay their bills. Often departing guests are in a great rush. The cashier must smile. It's important to be pleasant and courteous when taking someone's money. The cashier must be poised and ready to take complaints. Often the guests have "saved up" some complaint about their visit. When responding to complaints, the cashier must be polite and continue to sell, saying, "We're happy to have had you with us. We hope you'll return soon."

When the guest walks up to the front desk, the cashier calls the folio up on a computer terminal or pulls it from "the bucket." The

cashier then tells the guest the amount of the bill and asks, "Are these all of the charges?" This is done in case the guest incurred a recent charge, such as breakfast, that hasn't yet been posted. With computerized point-of-sale systems, all charges are likely to have already been posted.

The cashier accepts the payment and gives the guest a copy of the bill. The cashier then asks for the guest's room key. If the hotel is part of a chain, the cashier offers to help with making a reservation at the guest's next destination. A pleasant "goodbye" is then offered.

The cashier posts the payment to the guest's folio and the cash to the cash ledger. The folio is stored in the computer or returned to the bucket in a separate file for guests who have checked out. State laws vary as to how long registration information is kept, and to whom it is made available.

In-person group checkouts can be a nightmare. Often a group's room and taxes have been prepaid, but incidentals such as room service, bar bills, or telephone charges are not included in the package plan. This involves each member of the group communicating with the front desk or cashier. The pressure can be heightened by a tour bus noisily idling at the front door and tour leaders frantically trying to gather their charges. Conference checkout is usually done on an individual basis or the meeting planner may pay the accumulated bills. Regardless of the stress, hotel personnel must strive to make the last moments in the property pleasant for the guests.

POST CHECKOUT ACTIVITIES

For individuals and groups, the bellhop takes the luggage outside. The doorman opens the hotel and auto doors. The doorman may have already been asked to call a taxi or to get the guest's auto from the garage. The bellhop loads the luggage in the auto or bus and offers a pleasant "Goodbye, we hope you'll be staying with us again in the near future." The doorman also offers a final pleasant farewell.

Back inside the hotel, the cashier's computer notifies the front desk of the checkout. Telephone operators no longer have the guest's name listed, and housekeeping terminals show that the room is ready for cleaning. Noncomputer properties must convey this information verbally to the various departments.

The hotel hopes that the guests' stay has been pleasant and that this final impression of the hotel has conveyed efficiency and courtesy to them. If so, the guests will most likely return and recommend the establishment to friends.

TRENDS

As discussed in this chapter, the most obvious trend in the checkout process is computers replacing the face-to-face interaction between guests and front-desk personnel. Synthesized voices will communicate with guests in the checkout procedure. Sophisticated electronics provide instantaneous folio adjustments. Computers give accountants and management detailed records with few keystrokes. In the future smart cards with their vast amounts of hidden data will assure good credit risks for a property and will enable quick transfers of funds.

Computers should never totally replace goodwill that is generated by a hospitable host or hostess extending, "Thanks for staying here," or "Have a good trip." Neither should the opportunity to reserve for a next visit nor book a room at another chain affiliate be missed.

CHAPTER ACTIVITIES

FRONT-OFFICE OPERATIONS: ACCOUNTING AND CHECKING OUT

1. Mr. and Mrs. Page, for whom you filled out a reservation and a registration form, have been at the hotel for five days, April 1–5. On the sample folio, post the charges and credits and tally their total bill.

April 1	April 2	April 3
Room $48.00	Room	Room
Tax 5%	Tax	Tax
Beverages $3.25	Food $7.50	Beverage $4.85
Local phone 75¢	Local phone 75¢	Local phone 50¢
	Advance payment $75	Long distance $3.55

April 4	April 5
Room	Room
Tax	Tax
Valet $2.50	Food $6.75

Room No.	No. Persons	Rate	Arrival	Departure		
					No.	51114

NAME: _____

The
Wise Hotel

SIGNATURE: _____

Old Folio No.

Next Folio No.

DATE							
Balance Forward							
Room							
Tax							
Telephone (LOCAL)							
Telephone (L.D.)							
Laundry							
Rood							
Beverages							
Cash Disbursements							
Transfer							
TOTAL							
Cash Receipts							
Transfer							
Allowances							
BALANCE							

2. List the precautions to be used in cashing checks.

3. List the precautions to be used in processing credit cards.

4. Define the following:

   overstays

   walk-ins

   skippers

   sleepers

CHAPTER PROJECTS

1. Your instructor has materials for a night audit project. Fill out and cross-check the night auditor's spreadsheet.

2. Locate the nearest bank that exchanges foreign currency. Write a paper discussing their procedures and rate variations.

3. Discuss with friends and family their experiences in checking out of hotels. Describe the differences that you ascertain.

7 HOUSEKEEPING, ENGINEERING, AND SECURITY

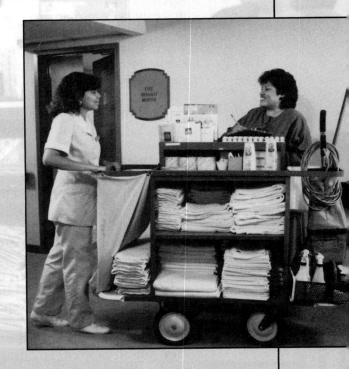

CHAPTER OUTLINE

LEARNING OBJECTIVES

After reading this chapter, you should be able to

- Write a job description for an executive housekeeper.
- Describe the job of room cleaners.
- Define the areas where the housekeeping and engineering departments overlap.
- List the duties of the chief engineer.
- Explain a property's security measures.

HOUSEKEEPING

The ***housekeeping department*** is responsible for the cleanliness, appearance, and condition of the entire hotel. This includes ***public areas*** (such as the lobby, public rest rooms, and meeting rooms) as well as individual guest rooms.

A hotel's income depends on the number of rooms occupied at any given moment. It is the housekeeping department's responsibility to efficiently keep as many rooms as possible in a ready condition. Information regarding ***ready rooms,*** those ready for a new guest, must be conveyed to the front office immediately, or a sale might be lost. With computerized communications systems, the housekeeping department can convey room availability to the front desk almost instantaneously.

The housekeeping department can also be responsible for more glamorous jobs such as interior decorating and arranging fresh flowers for VIPs. Don't think only of running a vacuum cleaner when you hear the word "housekeeping." An efficiently managed housekeeping department is vital to the smooth operation of a hotel.

BASIC DUTIES OF THE HOUSEKEEPING DEPARTMENT

Guest Rooms.   Cleaning guest rooms involves the following: Bed linen is changed daily, the furniture is dusted, ashtrays emptied, and the carpet vacuumed. The bathroom sink, toilet, tub, and floor are scrubbed. Clean towels are put in place. Supplies such as matches, soap, shampoo, tissue, and hotel literature are left.

The rooms must be kept in good repair. The executive housekeeper makes periodic checks for maintenance needs. For example, certain rooms might need to be closed for a day or so in order that they can be painted. The housekeeper keeps track of those rooms that need redecorating; for example, frayed bedspreads may need to be replaced. In some hotels, a maintenance request form is left on the night stand for the guests' convenience. This form is filled out and brought to the front desk for any nonurgent repairs.

Public Rooms.   Cleaning public rooms is almost a 24-hour job in a large hotel. Of course, the lobby must be kept spotless for that all-important first impression on the guests. Public restrooms need to be spot-cleaned throughout the day and into the night until all restaurants have closed and meetings have adjourned.

Outside Grounds.   The outside grounds of a hotel might be the responsibility of housekeeping, another separate department within the hotel, or an outside contractor. Keeping the shrubbery, grass, and

There's a problem!!!!

To notify the Housekeeping, Maintenance, or Engineering departments of a problem in your room, please drop this card at the front desk. We will correct the problem promptly.

Room No. _____　Date: _____

Description of problem:

_____

_____

_____

_____

_____

Sorry you were inconvenienced.

The Management

(For front office use)

Date: _____　Time received: _____

Department assigned: _____

Time dispatched to department:

Solution: _____

_____

_____

_____

Time and date resolved: _____

FIGURE 7-1

Card used by guests to request repairs or supplies

flower beds in trim condition is a big job. At resorts with pools and tennis courts, recreation departments will usually handle this cleaning and maintenance.

Special Requests. Special requests that are handled by housekeeping involve such things as setting up baby cribs or loaning hair dryers and irons. The department must keep an inventory of these items. The housekeeping department also is in charge of "lost and found" items.

In some hotels the housekeeping department also employs a repair or maintenance staff. Usually the need for repairs would be conveyed to the engineering department. Close coordination between the housekeeping department and the maintenance and engineering departments is a must.

HOUSEKEEPING PERSONNEL

Executive housekeepers must have excellent people skills since their staff is so large and diverse. In certain parts of the country it is helpful if executive housekeepers speak a second language since many workers may be immigrants. They also must be extremely organized, for they maintain an extensive inventory of supplies that must be ordered and kept on hand. Salaries for executive housekeepers in large hotels can be quite high.

The executive housekeeper hires a staff, which, depending on the size of the property, can consist of an assistant or several assistants and possibly a secretary. The housekeeping offices are usually located in or near the linen room—the heart of the housekeeping department. In a large hotel there is usually one supervisor for every two floors or for certain blocks of rooms. These supervisors, along with the executive housekeeper, inspect rooms that have been cleaned and those that are vacant to be sure they are ready. Larger hotels have checkers that inspect for the supervisors. These people spot-check behind the room cleaners for cleanliness and repairs.

The executive housekeeper acts as contractor for certain cleaning jobs. For example, due to the danger of exterior window washing, *requests for proposals (RIPs)* are sent out to several companies who then bid on the needs described. An annual contract may be in force for such deep cleaning as carpet shampooing.

With a computerized system, the executive housekeeper can check the status of each room hour by hour. The computer screen in Figure 7-2 shows seven rooms occupied and the number of nights the guests will remain. Nine rooms are on change (OC) or being cleaned and seven are ready, which is indicated by not having a notation. As rooms are cleaned, the executive housekeeper conveys this information to the front desk via the housekeeping department computer.

In the morning the executive housekeeper sends a rooms report to the front desk. From this a *discrepancy report* is made. This report coordinates with front-desk records which rooms are occupied. It shows if a room that is supposed to be vacant is in use, and also the

```
            DATE        0905--                    TIME  1:17:52  p.m.

    ROOM    STATUS          BED TYPE     NITES REMNG   MAID ASSIGNED
    Housekeeping Report
    **************************************************************
    1500  STAY            TUB 2DBL         2    .........................
    1501  STAY            TB  QUEEN        1    .........................
    1502          OC      TB  QUEEN        0    .........................
    1503                  TUB 2TWN         0    .........................
    1504          OC      TUB 2TWN         0    .........................
    1505  STAY            TUB DBL          1    .........................
    1506                  TUB 2TWN         0    .........................
    1507  STAY            TUB DBL          1    .........................
    1510                  TUB 2TWN         0    .........................
    1512          OC      TUB DBL          0    .........................
    1514                  2 TWINS          0    .........................
    1515                  DBL              0    .........................
    1516  STAY            DBL              4    .........................
    1517                  TB  2TW          0    .........................
    1600  STAY            TUB 2DBL         1    .........................
    1601  STAY            TB  QUEEN        1    .........................
    1602          OC      TUB DBL          0    .........................
    1603          OC      TUB 2TWN         0    .........................
    1604          OC      TB  QUEEN        0    .........................
    1605          OC      TUB DBL          0    .........................
    1606          OC      2 TWINS          0    .........................
    1607          OC      TUB DBL          0    .........................
    1610                  TUB DBL          0    .........................
```

FIGURE 7-2

Housekeeping report

opposite—if a room that is supposed to be occupied is vacant. The discrepancy is then thoroughly investigated. The evening rooms report summarizes ready rooms available for rent.

Room Cleaners

The majority of workers in the housekeeping department are *room cleaners.* They clean the guest rooms, the public areas including public rest rooms, and the executive offices. They work shifts and must perform up to the standards set by the establishment. Since they have contact with the guests, room cleaners should have pleasant personalities.

FIGURE 7-3

Most employees in the housekeeping department are room cleaners.

Checkers.   Checkers or supervisors can check the thoroughness of room cleaners, and new electronic devices can check their efficiency. One such monitor has the room cleaner dial on the room phone a code which gives such information as the room number and a personal identification. Upon leaving the room a "finished" or "ready" code is dialed. The executive housekeeper receives these messages on a computer and thus knows at all times the status of each room, as well as where the room cleaners are, and the time it takes them to do a job.

Room cleaners and checkers use the room inspection lists shown in Figure 7-4 to be sure they've completed the work. Notice these lists not only involve cleaning duties but also ask the cleaner to pinpoint structural problems and inventory shortages.

The rooms must be kept in good repair. The executive housekeeper makes periodic checks for maintenance needs. For example, certain rooms might need to be closed for a day or so in order that they can be painted. The housekeeper keeps track of those rooms that need redecorating; for example, frayed bedspreads may need to be replaced.

Laundry Personnel

There are two alternatives to linen procurement. Hotels may rent linens from large suppliers who deliver the sheets, pillowcases,

ROOM INSPECTION LIST
CLEANING CHECK

DO BEDS MEET THE FOLLOWING STANDARDS?	YES	NO
Made correctly	——	——
Pillows fluffed	——	——
Bedspread fresh and clean	——	——

DO FLOORS MEET THE FOLLOWING CRITERIA?		
Carpets vacuumed	——	——
Wood floors scrubbed	——	——

ARE THE FOLLOWING ITEMS FREE OF DUST?		
Desk tops	——	——
Dresser tops	——	——
Table tops	——	——
Headboard	——	——
Chair arms	——	——
Chair rungs	——	——
Tops of picture frames	——	——
Baseboards	——	——
Lamps and shades	——	——
Top of window frame	——	——
Window sills	——	——
Inside of drawers	——	——
Closet shelves	——	——
Telelphone	——	——

ARE THE FOLLOWING BATH ITEMS CLEAN?	YES	NO
Basin	——	——
Underside of basin	——	——
Pop-up stopper	——	——
Toilet seat, both sides	——	——
Tub/shower	——	——
Shower curtain	——	——
Floor tile	——	——
Is the toilet seat band in place?	——	——

DOES THE ROOM CONTAIN THE FOLLOWING ITEMS?		
Ten coat hangers	——	——
Room and bath trash cans	——	——
Three ashtrays	——	——
Matches	——	——
Soap	——	——
Towels	——	——
Washcloths	——	——
Tissue	——	——
Two rolls of toilet paper	——	——
Sanitary bags	——	——
Shoe shine cloth	——	——
Shampoo	——	——
Body lotion	——	——
Do not disturb sign	——	——
Rate card	——	——
Tent card	——	——
Postcards/stationery	——	——
Menu	——	——
Hotel events guide	——	——
Phone book	——	——
Bible	——	——
Glasses	——	——
Ice bucket	——	——

FIGURE 7-4

Room inspection list—cleaning check

ROOM INSPECTION LIST
MAINTENANCE CHECK

DO THE FOLLOWING ITEMS WORK PROPERLY?	YES	NO	DO THE FOLLOWING BATH ITEMS WORK PROPERLY?	YES	NO
Doors	___	___	Faucets	___	___
Windows	___	___	Toilet	___	___
Closet doors	___	___	Toilet seat	___	___
Drapes	___	___	Heat light	___	___
Locks	___	___	Shower enclosure	___	___

DO THE FOLLOWING ELECTRICAL ITEMS WORK PROPERLY?			DO UPHOLSTERED ITEMS MEET THE FOLLOWING CRITERIA?		
Light switches	___	___	Are chairs, etc., clean and unfrayed?	___	___
Bulbs	___	___	Is the bedspread in good condition?	___	___
Air conditioning	___	___	Is the mattress firm and turned?	___	___
Heating	___	___			
Filters	___	___	Are lampshades clean?	___	___
Television	___	___	Are rugs and carpeting clean and fresh?	___	___
Telephone	___	___			

CHECK OVERALL CONDITION OF ROOM	YES	NO
Is wall covering fresh?	___	___
Are walls free of nicks and scratches?	___	___
Is furniture in perfect condition?	___	___
Are windows free of cracks?	___	___
Do drapes open and close properly?	___	___
Are bulbs the proper wattage?	___	___
Do dresser drawers slide easily?	___	___
Are glass tops clean and unscratched?	___	___

FIGURE 7-4

Room inspection list—cleaning check *(continued)*

towels, tablecloths, and napkins that a hotel needs on a daily basis. Hotels using these suppliers are renting their linen needs. Instead of renting linens, a property might own the linen and care for it in its own laundry. Washing machines can handle up to 7,000 pounds of laundry per hour. If the hotel has its own laundry facility, the executive housekeeper's job is tremendously expanded and would involve supervising more employees, possibly including sewing personnel.

ENGINEERING

The *engineering department* plays a vital role in maintaining a quality product to sell to guests. It may be involved in daily maintenance as well as in highly technical areas. What do you think are the three most common calls made to the engineering department? They are requests for checking the air conditioning, adjusting the television reception, and unstopping a clogged drain or toilet. If these chores are not performed, the guest will be unhappy and certainly will never return.

DUTIES OF THE ENGINEERING DEPARTMENT

The engineering department is responsible for maintaining the facility's physical plant. Among other general duties the department must maintain the plumbing, the electricity, and the heating and air conditioning systems.

In thinking about the importance of the engineering department, consider what is involved in maintaining a hotel's plumbing. In an 800-room property, there are 800 toilets in the guest's rooms, plus many more in the public areas. There are two drains in each bath, one in the basin and one in the tub—that comes to 1,600 drains! No wonder one of the most common problem calls to engineering concerns plumbing.

Next think about the vastness of the electrical system in a large hotel. Not only must the electrical system be maintained, but the engineering department is also in charge of microphone or movie projector hook-ups for conferences. If a large trade show is being held with many exhibitors' booths, much time for setup is demanded from the engineering department.

The heating and air conditioning system is the third area involving the department. Most rooms have individual thermostats, each, of course, with its own temperament.

```
MAINTENANCE WORK ORDERS          12/07/--            11:55

5076 RM:    335 09/06/--    MISSING LAMP ON CORNER TABLE
5077 RM:    331 09/06/--    MISSING TABLE LAMP
5207 RM:    182 09/18/--    BED AND SUPPORT ON TABLE ARE LOOSE!!!!!
5314 RM:    481 09/23/--    PLASTIC SHADE OVER SINK IS CRACKED
5336 RM:        09/24/--    BACK STAIRWELL TOWER NEEDS REPAINTING
5386 RM:   9999 09/27/--    CEILING LAMP IN CONCOURSE IS MISSING A SHADE***
5551 RM:        10/12/--    SIGN BETWEEN 2 ELEVATORS, 4TH FL. NEEDS REPLACING
5707 RM:   9999 10/25/--    LEFT TOWER ELEVATOR'S EMERGENCY PHONE LID BROKEN
5719 RM:        10/26/--    INSIDE OF TOWER ELEVATOR NEEDS TO BE PAINTED
5727 RM:        10/26/--    NR 202, REPLACE WALLPAPER BETWEEN DOOR AND WINDOW
5739 RM:    333 10/27/--    FRAMEWORK MISSING AROUND ENTRANCE LIGHT IN CEILING
6011 RM:    662 11/22/--    REPLACE LAMPSHADE BY BED/BADLY STAINED
6017 RM:        11/22/--    NEED TO REPAINT "NO DIVING" NOTICE AT POOL
6036 RM:        11/23/--    SOAP DISPENSERS BROKEN IN WOMENS BATH/LOBBY
6070 RM:    107 11/26/--    NEEDS TUB DRAIN COVER
6072 RM:        11/26/--    RULES/REGS SIGN FRAMES NEED TO BE CHANGED TO FIT
6073 RM:        11/26/--    ON BACK OF DOOR, MANY ROOMS IN MAIN
6137 RM:        12/01/--    SOAP DISPENSERS MISSING, MENS ROOM, LOWER LOBBY
6138 RM:        12/01/--    SOAP DISPENSERS BROKEN, LADIES ROOM, LOWER LOBBY
6200 RM:    180 12/07/--    2 SPOTS ON CARPET, BOTTOM OF RT BED
6201 RM:    581 12/07/--    NEEDS TO BE SHAMPOOED
*** PRESS SPACE BAR FOR MORE***
```

FIGURE 7-5

Maintenance work orders

Routine upkeep of paint and upholstery might fall under either engineering or housekeeping. Whichever, you can see why close communication between these two departments is important. Figure 7-5 shows typical maintenance work orders. This is an inventory of work needed to be done in guest rooms and public areas. The chief engineer or executive housekeeper could study these and realize that they need lamps and might order them at a bulk rate. If several rooms need wallpapering, an outside contractor might be called in to do the work.

ENGINEERING PERSONNEL

The *chief engineer* in a large hotel supervises specialized crafts people and licensed engineers. For example, in a large hotel there would be skilled plumbers and an electrical engineer. In a smaller hotel people with general skills would be employed and they would be in charge of general maintenance of the small property.

Large renovations call for *outside contractors.* A group of painters might be employed so that a block of rooms could be refreshed more

quickly. The chief engineer also administers outside maintenance contractors on such items as elevators.

There is an anecdote about the chief engineer who couldn't repair his heating system. He called in an outside contractor who stayed in the boiler room five minutes listening to the system. The contractor then took out a hammer, hit one of the pipes three times, and the system turned on. He sent a bill for $750. When the chief engineer inquired why the bill was so high for only five minutes of his time, the contractor informed him that it cost $50 for his time, and $700 for knowing just where to strike.

This points out the importance of good personnel choices in engineering. The chief engineer must have good business sense in handling a mass of paperwork, making priority judgments, and working with contractors' bids.

SECURITY

Security involves protecting both guests and employees. The department promotes safety for both people and their property.

DUTIES OF THE SECURITY DEPARTMENT

Prevention of thievery is a foremost objective of the security department. This includes the loss of property of the hotel itself and of its guests and employees. This involves public spaces, guest rooms, private offices, and employee areas.

Public spaces may be monitored via closed circuit T.V. and/or by personal guards. In particular, parking areas are closely monitored, especially if they involve enclosed garages. The lobby area, meeting rooms, eating establishments, and public rest rooms are also monitored. Basically, guests have reason to expect safety from entry of their rooms and corridors leading to them. Each state mandates its trespass laws and all differ from one another. One of the most difficult situations is the definition of undesirables and course of action to be taken when they are on the premises. Here again, state laws give guidelines for such instances.

The security department is charged with advising the property on door locks that ensure that guest rooms are inaccessible to all but the renter. Key systems were discussed in Chapter 5. Security is usually in charge of the use of the emergency key. This key opens even double-

locked doors. Peepholes are a simple means of promoting basic room security.

A disclaimer that the hotel is not responsible for the loss of personal property is often seen on the rooming/registration card, or on the folder that contains the room key or card. Complicated law suits arise as to liability and negligence when personal property is lost. Safety deposit boxes are provided to guests in most properties. The security department establishes procedures for access to the boxes, which usually include signature cards and double keys. In-room safes are sometimes provided. Guests program their own combination to gain entry.

In addition, the security department is involved in establishing emergency procedures. These would involve fire detection, extinguishing equipment, and evacuation plans. Policies to follow in the event of a power failure or bomb threat are also designed by the security department. Security should hold periodic drills with employees for such situations. Medical emergency procedures are established by security.

PERSONNEL

Some properties choose to contract for their security. This can be even with off-duty policemen. An advantage of contracting is that little training is involved. A disadvantage is that with contracted security the property has less direct control. Even if contracted out, some employee is empowered as chief of security and oversees the operation.

TRENDS

More and more duties and responsibilities of the housekeeping, engineering, and security departments of a property will be taken over by contractual personnel. This reapportioning of the workforce is taking place in many businesses. Department heads will have fewer one-on-one personnel decisions to make, but will have to hone contract negotiation and mediation skills.

General housekeeping changes that are occurring revolve around the increased numbers of extended-stay, condo, and time-sharing accommodations. Daily room cleaning is often not offered in such situations, but kitchen cleanup is added to the task list. Initial food provisioning in longer term rentals will become an offered service. Major redecorating in condos and time-shares is periodically

ENVIROLODGE

The Wise Hotel is a participant in the world-wide **Envirolodge** initiative. This is a voluntary program of cooperation between lodging establish-ments and their guests. Together we can conserve air quality, water and energy resources.

How you can help:
* You can help save thousands of gallons of water and detergent. Replace towels on the towel rack to indicate, "I'll use it again." Place them in the tub to indicate, "Please exchange." Place this card on a pillow to indicate that the sheets not be changed. (Sheets are changed automatically after two nights and for new guests.)

* Energy is conserved by keeping the air conditioning and heat controls set at 70 degrees. When in use keep windows and doors shut.

Thank you for doing your part to save our environment!!

FIGURE 7-6

Some properties enlist guests in conservation efforts.

scheduled and may be provided by housekeeping departments. Some properties are even enlisting the guests' aid in conservation of resources (see Figure 7-6).

Engineering departments are under constant pressure to provide energy-saving ideas and proposals. These departments may be responsible for cost analysis, renovation time lines, and design solutions. A more health-conscious public is demanding things such as fresh air access and filtered water. Providing the mechanics for these types of needs are the responsibility of engineering.

Though not in wide use as yet, security becomes more automated with the advent of smart cards which will become the standard credit/debit card transfer medium. The smart card recognizes information embedded in a microchip, and such information can be used on card room lock systems. In addition to room access, parking garage entrance and egress, and even elevator activation can be controlled by such cards. Video monitoring in coordination with computer controls gives more power to security efforts.

CHAPTER ACTIVITIES

HOUSEKEEPING, ENGINEERING, AND SECURITY

1. You are the executive housekeeper for a 150-room motel located on a major interstate highway in a large city. It averages an 80 percent occupancy rate, with little variance between weekends and weekdays. Half of its guests are business travelers and half are vacation travelers. Business travelers tend to check out between 8 and 9 A.M. while vacation travelers often check out as early as 7 A.M. to go to their next destination.

   On an 8-hour shift a room cleaner can clean approximately 12 rooms per day. A checker or assistant housekeeper should check at least 4 rooms per day cleaned by each room cleaner. Ideally, room cleaners would be given a 40-hour week with two consecutive days off.

   a. How many cleaners will you need each day?

   b. How many checkers will you need?

   c. Draw up charts that show scheduling for the cleaners and checkers for a month.

2. Using the room inspection list shown in Figure 7-2, inspect your own bedroom and bath. Report your findings.

CHAPTER PROJECTS

1. Call a linen supply firm and find out the types of linens available, their frequency of deliveries, and their procedures for replacing worn linen. Report your findings to the class.

2. Discuss with the local police department the number and nature of calls received from lodging establishments in your area.

3. Talk with the engineering department of a hotel/motel in your area. Answer the following questions:

   a. How many people are employed in the department?

   b. What are the titles of the engineering department employees?

   c. What are the specialties of the employees?

   d. How many outside contractors are used?

   e. What are the outside contractors' specialties?

FOOD AND BEVERAGE DEPARTMENT

CHAPTER OUTLINE

LEARNING OBJECTIVES

After reading this chapter, you should be able to

- Give the titles of persons who work for the food and beverage manager.
- Describe a purchasing steward's duties.
- Give examples of food cost control in a hotel food and beverage operation.
- Give examples of beverage inventory and cost control.
- Explain types of service used in restaurants.

FOOD AND BEVERAGE DEPARTMENT ADMINISTRATION

The food and beverage (F & B) department of a hotel or motor inn is a large, complex department. Figure 8-1 illustrates an organizational chart for a hotel restaurant that seats approximately 250 people and has one large and one small banquet room. Many large hotels have two or three restaurants plus a bar and coffee shop. Food service outlets may be operated independently of the hotel. A restaurant and/or bar owner may rent space from a property. This might be a local enterprise or a well-known franchise. In such cases, in addition to monthly rental charges, a percentage of the income is paid to the hotel. The administrative function includes the activities of purchasing, receiving, taking inventory, and controlling. The purchasing and receiving stewards, along with the department controller, report to the F & B manager.

PERSONNEL

The *food and beverage manager* is the overall director of the department. This person is ultimately responsible for all department activities including administrative functions, food preparation, and serving guests. The food and beverage manager supervises all employees in the department including, in administration, the purchasing and receiving stewards, and the controller; in food preparation, the executive chef and the kitchen steward; and in service, the maitre d', the wine steward, and the banquet manager. Because the various jobs in the department overlap, close coordination between all personnel is needed.

PURCHASING

The *purchasing steward* buys all of the vegetables, fruits, meats, breads, and dry goods needed to produce the desired meals. The purchasing steward gets quotes and estimates from several suppliers, usually three, and makes judgments such as whether paying a higher price is worth better quality. The purchasing steward gets a forecast from the department controller and coordinates closely with the banquet manager to know the quantities to order.

Another responsibility of the purchasing steward is to make sure that fresh, dried, and canned foods are on hand to meet the restaurant's needs at all times. Fresh vegetables and fruits must be ordered daily; meats must be ordered roughly every three days. A par stock of staples, such as salt and sugar, must be kept on hand at all times.

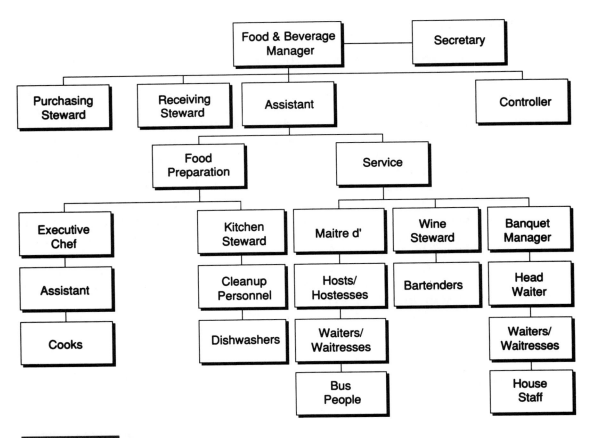

FIGURE 8-1

Organization chart for a hotel restaurant

The purchasing steward might suggest a daily special to the food and beverage manager when in-season foods are available inexpensively. Of course, the head chef, when "inspired" to make a special creation, would consult with the purchaser on availability of ingredients.

You learned in the chapter on housekeeping about the large linen supply companies that deliver clean napkins and tablecloths regularly to restaurants. This is also done by food suppliers. One company could furnish all meats and another could supply dried goods on a regular basis to the restaurant. Or one supplier might provide all the food needs of a restaurant. Some purchasing stewards and/or chefs pride themselves on personally choosing raw materials at fish markets or produce stands.

INVENTORY

The *receiving steward* is the quality-control link for the restaurant. This person not only checks that the quantity ordered has been sent and correctly charged, but also that the quality of what is delivered meets the restaurant's standards. The receiving steward directs the food either to the kitchen, the refrigerators, the freezers, or the storerooms and also properly tags and dates everything, including par staples. Food service generally operates under what is called *FIFO: first in–first out.* The barrel of flour bought four months ago is used before the barrel that was placed in inventory last month. This promotes less waste by ensuring that food doesn't exceed expiration dates. The purchasing steward must rotate the inventory shelf space to facilitate this.

Keeping track of inventory is a vital activity of the food and beverage department. Weekly inventories are made up from the paperwork received from the receiving steward and from storeroom and cold storage requisition slips. A physical inventory is conducted at least monthly. Just as in retail stores, computers now make this an easier job; but a "hands-on" count must still be done periodically to reveal waste or theft.

CONTROLLING

The food and beverage department controller checks invoices against receipts and may work with the general accounting office in paying bills. Another important function of the controller is to put out weekly and daily forecasts as to the number of guests who will be eating in the restaurant. The weekly forecast is adjusted daily according to the number of guests in the hotel and in conjunction with the banquet manager who knows what group meals are to be prepared.

The forecast is determined from records regarding how many people ate at the restaurant on the same date a year ago and statistics which indicate trends toward increased or decreased business for the restaurant. The forecast is used in all sections of the food and beverage department. For example, the maitre d' uses it to decide how many bus people will be needed for a given day. The purchasing steward uses it to determine how much to buy.

Food cost control is a primary function of the department controller, who keeps records of food sales and food purchases. There are wide fluctuations with adjustments for opening and closing inventories, but a monthly pattern can be established. If the food-cost ratio is

FIGURE 8-2

All employees who produce or prepare food in a restaurant kitchen report to the executive chef.

out of line, the controller traces the reason. The causes might be rises in purchasing prices, incorrect portion sizes, wasteful practices in receiving, spoilage, or pilferage. Menu prices are generally set by determining the cost plus the profit percentage desired.

FOOD PREPARATION

The *executive chef* is the manager of the food preparation division. Executive chefs are traditionally temperamental and want total charge of their kitchens. They are in charge of all people who produce

FIGURE 8-3

In large restaurants the preparation of elegant desserts is the responsibility of a pastry chef.

or prepare food. They work with the purchasing steward in ordering food. They deal with the controller in food-cost control which involves, for example, portion size and pricing. Excellent chefs are in demand and often command huge salaries.

In a large restaurant there are salad chefs, bakers, and any number of other cooks. The hiring and supervision of these employees is the executive chef's responsibility.

The *kitchen steward* is in charge of all else in the kitchen of a large restaurant. The kitchen steward has nothing to do with food preparation but is in charge of such activities as dish washing and sanitation work. The kitchen steward coordinates closely with the banquet manager in loaning china and silver to meeting rooms. He or she also may be in charge of purchasing linens and kitchen equipment.

SERVICE

As in all other aspects of a hotel, service is the key to restaurant success. Even with mediocre food, patrons will return to a restaurant for its excellent service.

RESTAURANT F & B SERVICE

The *maitre d'* or maitre d' hotel is the master of the hotel's food service, acting as supervisor of the dining room. Scheduling employees is one of the major responsibilities of the maitre d'. There may be a head waiter who is responsible for training the waiters, waitresses, and bus people to be efficient and polite.

Training in the style of service used is essential. The following are types of service:

Plate/American service—Food is prepared in the kitchen, placed on plates, and brought to diners.

Family/English service—Dishes of food are placed on the table and diners serve themselves.

Plate/Russian service—Waiters take serving dishes to tables and serve each diner a portion.

Tableside/French service—Food is prepared by the restaurant staff at individual tables and served to the diners.

The maitre d' deals with the kitchen steward obtaining linens, china, and silver for the dining room. The maitre d' and the executive chef rehearse the staff in knowing and being able to describe the house specials.

The *wine steward* not only is in charge of beverage servers, but usually has the responsibility for keeping track of inventory for alcoholic beverages. This employee also must keep abreast of trends in drinking; for example, since white wine and diet soda are now popularly requested, the wine steward must keep ample supplies of these beverages on hand. The wine steward might purchase all beverages or might work closely with the purchasing steward who does the ordering.

It is not unusual for the inventory value of liquor and wine alone to exceed $50,000. Because of this high value, pilferage is a great problem with liquor and wine inventories. Close control must be used even on the amount of liquor poured per drink. Bartenders are closely monitored. When banquet bars are set up in meeting rooms, the amount of liquor needed is estimated and issued for that

FIGURE 8-4

Excellent service will make patrons want to return to a hotel's restaurant.

particular event. The unused bottles are returned to inventory, but opened bottles are "lost" though they are paid for in the total price of the event.

Although in the past, quality restaurant service in hotels has been overlooked by many travelers, today many properties are contributing prime dining experiences for patrons. The goal is to increase repeat business. In addition, an excellent restaurant can build a local community reputation which in turn attracts banquet sales, thus room-night revenue.

NONRESTAURANT F & B SERVICE

Room service, at a full-service property, plays a vital part. A room-service menu must be devised, food preparers must be scheduled for

Our chef thinks each season should have a taste all its own.

At the Corinthian, a change of seasons is cause for celebration. Because that's when nature replenishes its food basket with seasonal bounty from the farms, orchards and waters of Maryland. We use these fresh ingredients as inspiration for many of the dishes that help create one of the finest dining experiences in Annapolis. Dine where great taste is always in season. Reservations suggested. FREE valet parking.

the **Corinthian**

At Loews Annapolis Hotel, 126 West Street, Annapolis, MD 21401 • *410-263-1299*

FIGURE 8-5

A hotel might advertise its outstanding restaurant not only to travellers, but to the local population. *The Loews Annapolis Hotel.*

the hours that the service is offered, and bell-staff for delivery must be available. Bar accessibility must be arranged. After a tiring day, many business travelers rely on relaxing in their room with food and drink. The F & B department of a property analyzes, from a cost-effectiveness viewpoint, the amount of room service to be offered.

In larger properties there may be a separate catering division or department. Usually the F & B manager carries overall responsibility for its operation. The F & B or catering department is responsible for food service at meetings and conferences. It might set up for coffee and snack breaks during meetings. A conference might request box lunches to be taken off-site for its attendees. A meeting with a tight, busy agenda might ask that a sandwich bar be set up in the lobby or near meeting rooms for quick meals.

There is always close coordination between F & B and sales. See the next chapter for more information on the banquet/catering function.

Food service in a restaurant is a vital area of income to the hotel. It is a major area which can make or break the reputation of a hotel/motel.

TRENDS

Large properties today are recognizing the revenue potential of food and beverage departments. As the number of rooms in a property grows, so must the number of eating possibilities within that property increase. There is a trend toward theme and/or ethnic restaurants being designed for hotels.

Menu choices are embracing the "healthy food" movement. A vegetarian entrée is usually included on menus. Meeting planners study the research on which food items provide energy instead of dozing when served for lunch.

Fast-food take-out and delivery systems cut somewhat into hotel food-service revenues. Domino's and other delivery personnel are seen on in-house phone lines in hotel lobbies, contacting guests for pickup. Some large properties get a bite of this business by renting space to such operations.

In many countries, the best restaurants are located in large hotels. More and more hotels are attempting to establish fine restaurant operations. Some achieve five fork, or five star, status which ensures local and repeat visitor clientele.

CHAPTER ACTIVITIES

FOOD AND BEVERAGE DEPARTMENT

1. Filet mignon is tomorrow's special. Name all of the food and beverage employees who must cooperate to get the meal before the diners. Tell what each person did with or for the filet mignon dinners.

2. List vegetables and meats/fish that would be in abundant quantity this month and that should be included in a menu. Research and write down what dishes might be made from these ingredients.

3. In two different dictionaries look up and define the word *steward*. Explain how the definition applies to the terms "purchasing steward," "receiving steward," and "wine steward."

CHAPTER PROJECTS

1. Talk to an executive chef and report to the class on his or her background and training.

2. Ask a purchasing steward to let you see the week's shopping list. Get permission to show the list to your class.

3. Investigate how many wholesale food distributors there are in your area.

9

SALES AND MEETING PLANNING

LEARNING OBJECTIVES

After reading this chapter, you should be able to

- Describe the function of the sales department.
- Describe the function of the catering/banquet department.
- Trace which departments of the hotel/motel are involved in banquet preparation.
- List sources of group business for a hotel/motel.
- Explain how a hotel/motel advertises.

The profit or loss of revenue of a motel/hotel depends on the number of rooms rented at any given time. Renting these rooms means selling them. Since the *sales department* of a property is responsible for selling the rooms, naturally, it is a vital division. In addition to selling rooms, the entire hotel product includes selling food and beverage, space for meetings, and recreational facilities. The job of those in the sales office is to bring increased business hence profits, to the hotel. They strive for more rooms rented at the highest rates possible, more dinners served, and more meeting rooms rented.

The sales staff in a small property most likely will be a sales manager and a secretary. Larger establishments, of course, have at least three people actively selling and might have an international division as well. Sales fall into two categories: group and individual. The aim is to sell sleeping rooms and meeting rooms. Group sales are then further subdivided into two types: meetings and packages.

MARKETING

Advertising, direct mail, publicity, and public relations are basic to the marketing, or selling, of any product. The sales office formulates the advertising for the hotel. Of course, if the property is part of a chain, only local advertising is needed. Sometimes the food and beverage department is responsible for the restaurant and bar advertising, and the sales department handles room and meeting space advertising. Most often an advertising agency designs the ad campaign and recommends what *media* to use. It might be newspapers, magazines, or broadcasts.

Brochures for individual, group, and internal sales must be prepared by the sales department. A direct mail campaign may be implemented. Multiple-page packets of information for meeting planners are designed. These would contain such information as the hotel's amenities and location, dimensions and capacity of meeting rooms, sample menus, and types of available guest rooms. Again, the sales office might use a sales promotion agency to design and write these brochures, or they may be done "in-house." Posters and signs for internal sales also must be produced.

The sales department also handles publicity, which may be considered free advertising. If a famous movie star stays at a property, for example, and the newspapers print the name of the hotel, it is worth thousands of dollars in print advertising. News releases are sent to newspapers on such items as personnel changes or major renovations. Radio and television stations are notified about events such as trade

shows. Public relations activities involve becoming active within the community. Certain properties are primary members of a city or region's *conference and visitor bureau (CVB).* These are organizations with dues-paying members from various businesses that benefit from tourism. In addition to accommodations facilities, attractions, restaurants, and tour companies are members. Joint efforts are made to lure travelers to the area. Participation by hotel staff in charitable events also puts the name of the property before the public in a positive manner.

In order to direct marketing activities, the sales department relies on research from the controller and the general manager regarding the best days of the week and the best months of the year for business. The night auditor, as stated in Chapter 6, compiles figures at the end of each day. These help sales and management to make projections. These projections are important for staffing, ordering linen supplies, and food purchasing. Percentages are derived for overstays, understays, walk-ins, no-shows, and number of reservations. Using formulas, *forecasts* can be reasonably accurate as to the number of guests to be housed on any given day. Chapter 4 discusses yield management statistics that are vital to the sales staff. Decisions on the availability of rooms and prices charged are based on yield management predictions.

The sales department should continually research why the hotel's guests are there. The staff needs to know if the guests are there on business or pleasure. How long the average guests stay and where they are from are also vital statistics. Whether the guests arrive by car or plane is important as well.

Why a guest chooses the particular property is vital information. The front desk or reservationist can assist my merely asking where the guest heard of the property. The registration card can include a simple question:

"How did you hear about our property?"

_____   Chain

_____   Travel agent

_____   Hotel representative

_____   Passing by

_____   Friend

_____   Yellow Pages

_____   Advertisement

_____   Other

Many hotels find out this type of information, as well as how to improve services and facilities, by placing questionnaires or "report cards" in each room. Guests are asked to fill them out and leave them in their rooms for housekeeping to turn in to management, or guests give them to the front desk when checking out.

GROUP SALES

Group sales are sales of more than one sleeping room or of one or more meeting rooms. A group sale might include selling a meeting room for the Twin Rivers Garden Club luncheon, or selling every sleeping room in the hotel to 500 members of the American Bar Association attending a convention. Cities with large convention centers hold events that place guests in many properties within the town. Group sales may also involve parties, weddings, bar mitzvahs, and graduations. Some hotels profit greatly from the wedding reception business.

TYPES OF GROUPS

MEETINGS

A meeting may be called a *convention,* a *conference,* a *seminar,* or any name invented by the group holding it. The size and "personality" of the group may vary widely. For example, compare the nature of the National Mary Kay Cosmetic Convention to a county CPA seminar.

In order to host meetings and conventions, a hotel must have adequate meeting rooms or be located near a large convention center. Some hotels depend on conventions for the majority of their business. For example, the Shoreham in Washington, D.C., and the Sherman House in Chicago receive over 60 percent of their dollar volume from conventions.

Resorts in such areas as San Juan and Honolulu are seeing more and more convention business. Hotels and motor inns near major airports are seeing a great increase in convention business, particularly in medium-size meetings or seminars. Today many organizations holding conventions are including the entire family in their planning. It is estimated that 60 to 75 percent of convention goers are accompanied by their spouses.

What are the sources of these meetings? Associations, companies, fraternal organizations, common interest groups, professional organ-

izations, and political groups, to name a few, all hold meetings in hotels for one reason or another.

Associations.   There are thousands of personal and professional *associations* in the United States and around the world. There is a trade association for every industry. We've all been amazed to hear of some of the specialized groups which hold meetings, for example, the Association of Yellow Pansy Growers, or the National Association of Pickle Packers. The groups have annual conventions for all of their members and often hold regional meetings as well. Some groups meet quarterly.

Companies.   Large companies, many of which support smaller companies, are holding more meetings than ever before. An example would be the Ford Motor Company holding a meeting for a group of its distributors. Also, some companies award top sales representatives *incentive travel,* or vacation awards, often in conjunction with sales meetings.

Fraternal organizations.   Fraternal organizations sometimes hold meetings at hotels. These might be the monthly Lions Club luncheon, a Greek sorority national meeting, or Kiwanis International holding a convention for thousands.

Common Interest Groups.   Common interest groups include garden clubs, sports booster clubs, even science fiction fan clubs or Hummel figurine collectors. These groups meet to compare and share materials on their common interest.

Professional Organizations.   These usually are made up of groups of lawyers, doctors, CPAs, or other skilled professionals. Their meetings might center around the presentation of scholarly papers or research that has been done in the particular field. Trade shows are often held in conjunction with these meetings. For example, textbook trade shows are staged at teachers' associations meetings.

Political Groups.   The National Democratic and Republican conventions constitute two of the largest gatherings in the United States. Only a handful of cities can accommodate these conventions. For these major conventions all hotel space in the chosen city is blocked. On a smaller scale the county's political parties might also hold meetings.

Trade Shows.   *Trade shows* are often held in conjunction with conventions, or they can be held without a formal organized meeting. At a trade show connected with the American Medical Association, for

FIGURE 9-1

Some trade shows are held in conjunction with formal meetings, whereas others are held for the sole purpose of exhibiting the industry's wares to the buying public.

example, pharmaceutical companies, medical supply companies, and a variety of other commercial businesses set up displays and exhibits. An example of a trade show not connected with a meeting would be some of the large travel shows where travel agents, wholesalers, and destinations exhibit and invite the public to attend. These are usually organized by professional commercial exhibit organizations. Keep in mind that even though a trade show might not involve an association, all the exhibitors require lodgings and usually stay at the hotel where the exhibit is held.

Mini-exhibits.   The mini-exhibits held in hotels/motels are individual company shows or auctions. The oriental rug dealers who rent meeting rooms to display their merchandise and advertise in the local paper for a showing are prime examples of the mini-exhibit. These exhibits provide a property income for a meeting room that might otherwise be empty, particularly on weekends at commercial hotels. They also bring people to the hotel who may decide to have dinner there.

TOUR GROUPS

The second type of group sales is accomplished through package plans organized by ***tour operators.*** Tour operators deal with the trans-

portation, accommodations, and sightseeing facets of travel. *Package plan* refers to a trip or travel arrangement that involves two or more components of tourism. For example, a package might include air and hotel arrangements. These would be offered together under a single price. Packages might include some or all meals. They might include *transfers* to and from the airport to the property. The transportation and the accommodations are the largest portion of any package.

A hotel sales manager's dream would be to have a tour operator block 50 rooms for a group tour that arrives each week. Even a remote motel between Atlanta and New Orleans might be the stop over for such a tour.

MAKING THE GROUP SALE

How do hotel sales offices reach the organizations that buy group accommodations? One way is through mass mailings conducted by the hotel's sales staff. Large hotels also have brochures directed to group business that describe their facilities for meetings.

Mailing lists can be made up by carefully reading newspapers to find out which organizations hold meetings. The American Society of Association Executives has mailing lists of its members.

Additionally, there are several different nationwide associations of meeting planners. Businesses on the local, regional, and state level are sources of potential meetings. Certainly working with the local CVB, chamber of commerce, and state tourism office will help identify meeting prospects. These organizations feed leads generated by advertising or general inquiries to various properties. The sales staff can then contact the potential group business. These offices will also help in making presentations to persuade large groups or associations to come to a property. If a meeting is so large that it uses several properties within a town or area, a CVB might act as a housing bureau, referring or handling reservations. The American Society of Travel Agents 1999 World Congress held in Strasbourg, France, expected 6,000 delegates to be placed in 80 hotels. Central reservations in such instances are required.

Close contact with tour operators is helpful in establishing or maintaining package tour business. There are tour operator associations that hold trade fairs where various destinations, hotels, and other tour-related services can exhibit.

A way in which smaller group sales can be stimulated is by writing a letter to those involved when an engagement announcement appears in the papers. Small membership organizations, such as the Lion's club, can be identified from the newspaper and perhaps offered a permanent meeting space at reduced rates.

When potential business is identified, sales calls are made. For those in the sales department, standard training in sales methods is helpful. Knowing how to turn features into benefits, recognize buying signals, and close a sale are basics in group sales.

AFTER THE SALE

The work of the sales department doesn't stop with the closing of the sale. Contracts showing the exact room, menu, and number expected are filled out by the sales representative and the group representative. Figure 9-2 illustrates a typical sales agreement for a meeting.

Coordination by sales with all departments in the hotel is the key to successful group functions. The front desk must be given blocked room information and be told the group rate being charged. Food and beverage, housekeeping, and hngineering also must be notified concerning their duties to make a successful meeting and thereby generate repeat business. When the sales department completes the contract in a larger hotel/motel, they would then turn the client over to the catering/banquet department.

SERVICING GROUPS: CATERING/BANQUET DEPARTMENT

Once the sale for a group meeting or meal is made, the ***catering/ banquet department*** takes over the organization and planning of the function. Think what a fulfilling job it would be to help an excited couple plan their wedding reception. For banquets or meetings, details such as the number of people at each table, placement of the head table, name tags, decorations, and microphones are involved. Large properties that schedule many meetings have personnel that are assigned to assist specific groups in making such decisions. The title used varies but often is ***convention services manager (CSM)*** or ***coordinator.*** Sometimes the catering/banquet department must assist with meeting details.

MENU PLANNING

The catering department works closely with the executive chef in planning menus for various events. Figure 9-3 shows a typical banquet menu or choice of meals that the catering department offers. With the client, a menu is chosen and thereby the price is determined.

Gateway Resort **EVENT ORDER**

EVENT ORDER NUMBER _02986_

ROOM _ADMIRAL RANSOM_   **FUNCTION** _CONFERENCE/LUNCH_

DATE OF EVENT _MAY 12, 20--_   **DAY** _WEDNESDAY_

NUMBER EXPECTED _135_   **NUMBER GUARANTEED** _125_

PRICE PER COVER _$12.00_   **ROOM RENTAL FEE** _$50.00_   **SET-UP CHARGE** _N/A_

NAME OF ORGANIZATION _TOURISM EDUCATORS_   **PHONE** _555-1111_

ADDRESS _123 BROAD STREET, NEW YORK, NY_

EVENT CONTACT _GEORGIANNA THOMAS_   **HOTEL CONTACT** _PHIL LATOUR_

METHOD OF PAYMENT _CHECK_   **DEPOSIT** _$50_

NAME OF ACTIVITY _QUARTERLY MEETING_   **BOOKED BY** _SS_   **DATE** _3/2/--_

MEETING ROOM
TIMES _9 AM_   **UNTIL** _4 PM_
SET-UP REQUIREMENTS:

    SLANTED SCHOOLROOM

FOOD FUNCTIONS
TIMES _12:30 PM_   **UNTIL** _1:30 PM_
SET-UP REQUIREMENTS:

      CIRCULAR

MENU

    SEE ATTACHED
    $9.50/

COFFEE BREAKS _10:30 AM_

    W/ DANISH @ $2.50/

BAR/HORS D'OEUVRES

    CASH BAR
    SET-UP $20.00

ADD A 15% SERVICE CHARGE TO ALL FOOD AND BEVERAGE PRICES.

I have read the above contract and the hotel's Catering Policies and Procedures printed on the reverse side and agree to the terms and conditions. This booking will remain tentative, subject to cancellation by the hotel, until this contract is signed and received by the hotel. Please sign and return one copy to Midwestern Inns' Gateway Resort.

_____   _____
(Sign Name)   (Print Name)   (Hotel Representative)

_____   _____
(Date)   (Date)

FIGURE 9-2

Hotel sales agreement for a meeting

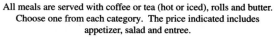

BANQUET MENU   The Wise Hotel

All meals are served with coffee or tea (hot or iced), rolls and butter.
Choose one from each category. The price indicated includes
appetizer, salad and entree.

APPETIZERS

Fresh fruit medley: Seasonal fruit topped with shredded coconut

Tomato juice: Served with celery stick and pepper sauce

Orange juice: Served with a splash of Grand Marnier

SALADS

Garden green tossed salad: Mixed greens topped with your
choice of dressing

Spinach salad: Fresh spinach topped with bacon and egg

Waldorf salad: Crisp apples, raisins, and nuts

ENTREES

Prime rib with twice baked potato au gratin	$22.98
Pork tenderloin au jus with oriental rice	$17.98
Filet of flounder dijon with baked potato	$15.98
Chicken chablis with grapes and wild rice	$15.98

DESSERTS
(Please add price to entree cost)

Key lime pie	$3.00
Rainbow sherbet	$2.50
Dessert cart: An assortment of cakes and pies	$3.25

Please add 5% state sales tax to the cost of the meal
Please add 15% gratuity to the cost of the meal
Menu and prices subject to change

FIGURE 9-3

Typical banquet menu

ROOM SETUP

The catering department explains to the client the room size and the possible setup arrangements (or styles of seating) available. Some possible options include lecture, classroom, or circular tables for dinners. Figure 9-4 illustrates such seating styles. In addition, the type and color of the linens are chosen, and the size and placement of the head table is decided. The catering department may employ a ***house staff*** to do the heavy work of setting up meeting or dining rooms, or these employees might work for the housekeeping department.

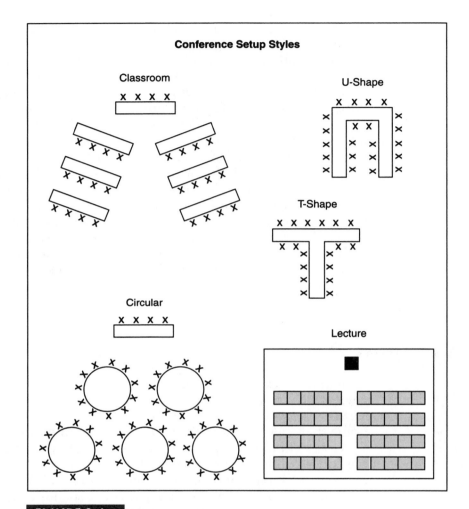

FIGURE 9-4

Conference setup styles

Equipment needs, such as film projectors, VCRs, and microphones, are discussed and arranged for by the catering department. When such equipment is used, the engineering department might be called in to do the "hook up." Some facilities charge extra for such services; others do not.

SPECIAL SERVICES

The catering department might be called upon to provide or subcontract for other amenities for a meeting, such as music in the form of

live bands or tapes; it might also be able to provide flowers or other decorative items for the event.

At a wedding reception held last June, the bride and groom, who were on a limited budget, chose to omit flowers in order to keep wedding costs down. The catering department assured them they could provide a centerpiece for their buffet table. Fortunately, a close friend of the couple went immediately to the reception hotel after the wedding service and discovered a plastic Rudolph the Red-Nosed Reindeer in the center of the buffet table! Disaster was averted when, after a quick discussion with the catering department, Rudolph was replaced with a sailboat. Though not ideal, the sailboat was much more appropriate as the groom was in the Navy.

The catering department acts as the conductor of an orchestra. It brings all the elements together to produce an event, working closely with the sales, food and beverage, housekeeping, and engineering departments. A willingness to work odd hours and a mind for detail can open the door to a most interesting career in this field.

INDIVIDUAL SALES

Individual sales are made primarily through repeat business—those guests that return to the property. This is accomplished through service. The guests must be impressed by the hotel. They must feel so at home that they wouldn't dream of trying another hotel.

Hotels should keep *profiles* on repeat guests, particularly those using concierge floors. Profiles would include information such as type of room preferred, method of payment used, and the need of transportation, business services, or valet. Using such information to save the guest time and certainly using the guest's name produce many return visits. The entire hotel staff is involved in the capacity of sales manager to influence repeat business. Chapter 2, "The Hospitality Business and You," and Chapters 4 through 6 on front-office operations discuss at length the "service equals repeat sales" theory.

Frequent-user programs have flourished in the last 10 years. For each night a guest stays at a property, points are given. After the points total a certain amount, a free night is earned. This establishes brand loyalty on the part of individual travelers. Most large chains have such programs, and some are tied in with airline frequent-flier plans.

Internal sales are an offshoot of individual sales. We discussed this in Chapter 4, when while rooming the guest, the bellhop had a casual conversation about the hotel restaurant being excellent.

Some hotel restaurants suffer from a misconception that their food isn't as good as that of the stand-alone restaurant a mile down the highway. Elevator ads showing a delicious meal or the elegant dining room may help to overcome this. Golf or tennis club memberships also are internal sales that might be made. In each room brochures describing the hotel's amenities further internal sales.

TRENDS

Several years ago there was widespread worry that telecommunications or videoconferencing would lessen the group-meeting business of hotels. This has not proven true. There are some companies that are equipped to videotape a meeting and simultaneously transmit it to be received at the home office or by other interested parties. Obviously this means hotel room-nights are not being utilized. Some properties have installed the equipment necessary for such transmissions. Fortunately for the industry, the success of such has been limited. Perhaps the reason is people want face-to-face interaction. Perhaps typical business travelers enjoy different atmospheres more than is professed.

More and more cities are jumping on the conference center bandwagon. The goal is to bring in more tourists, which in turn spend money in the region. This is, of course, advantageous to all the properties within the area since attendees at conference center events must have lodgings.

More meeting planners are contracting with local-event coordinators for meeting activities. Entertainment and/or sightseeing may be organized by professionals at an area. There are several schools that offer programs for those who want to become meeting planners or event coordinators. There are certifications that can be obtained through professional meeting planner organizations.

As organizations and businesses become more international in scope, more travelers from overseas are attending meetings. Knowledge of a second language is helpful, not only in the sales and catering departments, but by all staff at convention hotels.

CHAPTER ACTIVITIES

SALES AND MEETING PLANNING

1. The Sands Hotel is located in Bueno Beach, Florida. It is on beachfront property and has 250 rooms. There is an outdoor swimming pool, a tennis court, and golf course. There is a beautiful lobby and front-desk area. A poolside restaurant and bar serves breakfast, lunch, and dinner.

   Two large rooms can be combined and used for conventions or for large meetings seating theater-style up to 700 people. These same rooms can be used for banquet-style dinners for 400 people. A great deal of the hotel's business is meeting and banquet service.

   John George, executive secretary of the State Association of Piling Contractors, approaches you, the sales manager, about holding an annual dinner at your hotel on May 15. His address is 5445 Flintlock Road, Baltimore, MD 21122-1343, and his phone number is 301-555-5666. He guarantees 350 guests. He wants an open bar for one hour, 6:30–7:30 p.m. He wants to keep the cost at $30.00 per person.

   Fill out Event Order (Figure 9-2) using the sample menu (from Figure 9-3). Fill it out by role-playing with a classmate. Don't forget gratuities, taxes, and special needs such as a microphone or flowers. Use the Event Order given on page 161.

Gateway Resort   EVENT ORDER

EVENT ORDER NUMBER _____

ROOM _____   FUNCTION _____

DATE OF EVENT _____   DAY _____

NUMBER EXPECTED _____   NUMBER GUARANTEED _____

PRICE PER COVER _____ ROOM RENTAL FEE _____ SETUP CHARGE _____

NAME OF ORGANIZATION _____   PHONE _____

ADDRESS _____

EVENT CONTACT _____   HOTEL CONTACT _____

METHOD OF PAYMENT _____   DEPOSIT _____

NAME OF ACTIVITY _____   BOOKED BY _____ DATE _____

MEETING ROOM
TIMES _____   UNTIL _____
SETUP REQUIREMENTS:

COFFEE BREAKS

FOOD FUNCTIONS
TIMES _____   UNTIL _____
SETUP REQUIREMENTS:

MENU

BAR/HORS D'OEUVRES

ADD A 15% SERVICE CHARGE TO ALL FOOD AND BEVERAGE PRICES.

I have read the above contract and the hotel's Catering Policies and Procedures printed on the reverse side and agree to the terms and conditions. This booking will remain tentative, subject to cancellation by the hotel, until this contract is signed and received by the hotel. Please sign and return one copy to Midwestern Inns' Gateway Resort.

_____   _____   _____
(Sign Name)   (Print Name)   (Hotel Representative)

_____   _____
(Date)   (Date)

2. Write a survey to give to guests that will provide information that the sales department would find useful.

3. List 20 organizations in your area that hold meetings.

4. Write a letter to one of these organizations inviting them to meet at the Sands Hotel as described in Activity 1.

CHAPTER PROJECTS

1. Bring in hotel advertisements from three hotels.

2. Write a report on standard sales techniques, as discussed in this chapter.

3. Obtain copies of sales materials from a hotel in your area.

10 ACCOMMODATIONS:
REFERENCES AND RATINGS

CHAPTER OUTLINE

I. *Accommodation Information Sources*
Personal Recommendations
Advertising
Tour Brochures
Travel Guides

II. *Hotel Reference Books*
The *Official Hotel Guide*
OAG Business Travel Planner

III. *The Internet*

LEARNING OBJECTIVES

After reading this chapter, you should be able to

- List the most popular hotel/motel reference books.
- Research location, price, and ratings of major hotels throughout the world.
- Learn how to make reservations with major hotels throughout the world.
- Use the Internet to make accommodation reservations.

Guests may make hotel reservations in several ways. A guest may merely walk in and request a room. A direct telephone call to a property, a call to a 1-800/888 number to the chain reservation system, or a travel agent, airline, or tour operator might make the reservation. Today reservations may be made directly through the Internet to individual properties.

First, the consumer must have chosen a suitable property. There are several methods of not only finding the names of suitable properties at a given destination, but also of obtaining detailed information and instructions on how to make reservations there.

Basic sources of hotel information are

- recommendations from friends and acquaintances
- advertisements in magazines, newspaper, or broadcast media
- tour brochures
- travel guides
- hotel reference books
- the Internet

ACCOMMODATION INFORMATION SOURCES

RECOMMENDATIONS

"Stay downtown on the square at the Hotel Marquessa and ask for the corner room facing the cathedral and the zocalo." "A great hotel is the Maison Blanc, right in the French Quarter, and priced around $65." Some of the best recommendations on hotels come from word of mouth. Friends, acquaintances, and business colleagues give first-hand, frank information on properties within given areas.

ADVERTISING

Primarily large chains advertise in national media. Usually, ads seen in magazines, newspapers, and TV, and those heard on radio, feature the advantages of the chain on a whole, not individual properties. Most often a 1-800/888 number is given to book a room, and one calls a central reservation center. You will seldom see an ad for a hotel in your hometown, because its market is not the local populace.

TOUR BROCHURES

Brochures often list and describe various properties in an area. Such booklets may be published by the convention and visitor's bureau in

your area. These may list local hotels with addresses and phone numbers. Tour operators also print brochures that feature their packages. Usually a choice of hotels is offered and a brief description given. In most cases the price of a package tour can depend on your choice of a hotel.

TRAVEL GUIDES

Travel tour guides are found in abundance in bookstores. Most often these feature cities, states, regions, or countries. They usually contain maps and give general information concerning a destination. Sightseeing attractions and self-guided tours are recommended in these books. The guides list and give suggestions on accommodations and restaurants in an area. These do not try to be all-comprehensive, but list accommodations according to their readership audience. Guides may be directed to specific types of travelers. A huge variety reflect special interest, such as ecology or traveling with children.

Reference books and guides often rank accommodations and restaurants. The ranking system may be originated by the publisher, or sometimes the ranking used is that endorsed by a country. The basic star ranking is as follows:

*	Good, better than average
**	Very good
***	Excellent
****	Outstanding
*****	One of the best in the country

Thus we hear, "It's a five-star hotel." An example of a national ranking system is France. There the secretary of state for tourism ranks properties with one to five stars indicating Luxury, Top Class, Very Comfortable, Good, or Plain but Fairly Comfortable. Some references use dollar signs ($) to indicate prices of properties. $$$$$ would denote a very expensive property.

Frommer's guides originated in the 1960s with *Europe on $5.00 a Day*. The many Frommer guides that are published continue to emphasize budget accommodations and restaurants. Adjunct publications are Frommer's *Frugal Traveler's Guides*. These further emphasize budget travel (www.frommers.com).

Let's Go guides are primarily written by reader contribution. *Lonely Planet* guides make many suggestions for student and backpacking travelers.

Fodor Guides are very popular and feature countries throughout the world. Fodor Travel Publishing and the Mobil Oil Company formed a partnership and now publish many guides. *Mobil Travel Guides* divide the United States into regions, giving detailed information on highway systems, attractions, hotels, and restaurants for each region. Fodor is also in partnership with a large Internet Web site: Preview Travel. Accommodation suggestions on the site are from Fodor research.

HOTEL REFERENCE BOOKS

Hotel reference books are found primarily in travel agencies. These are useful, particularly in finding out specific information on hotel/motel properties. These too may have a method of ranking properties by quality. Travel reference books give more detailed information than the other sources.

For instance, a traveler client might want to know how far a particular hotel is from the airport. Many listings have locator maps that show the exact distance from the airport to all the hotels in the area. Does a property have a swimming pool? This information is also available in many reference books. Certainly the listings are invaluable in obtaining addresses, phone numbers, reservation representatives, and commission information.

THE OFFICIAL HOTEL GUIDE

The *Official Hotel Guide,* published annually, contains over 30,000 listings of hotels, business facilities, resorts, and inns. The three-inch thick directory covers the Americas, Canada, Asia, and Europe. Over 350 city maps are included in the index. Number of rooms, amenities, and price range are among the detailed information given. Hotel chain or representative affiliation and reservation information are supplied.

OAG BUSINESS TRAVEL PLANNER

Three editions are published of the invaluable *OAG Business Travel Planner: North American, European, and Asia Pacific.* The Caribbean is included in the North American edition. These are issued four times a year by the Reed Travel Group. These guides provide excellent information on each city and feature city and airport maps for major sites. Governmental entry requirements, embassy and consulate locations,

general weather information, and major attractions for foreign countries are given. The North American edition also contains a listing of colleges, universities, and military installations.

The *OAG Travel Business Planners* vary slightly in that the North American edition lists alphabetically by city, while the European and Pacific Asia editions list by country and then by city.

Figure 10-1 illustrates listings from the Pacific Asia edition of the *OAG Business Travel Planner.* In looking at the listing, you see an airplane symbol to the right of the name of the city. This indicates that Sydney is "on-line" with its own airport. The area code (AC) or city dialing code (CDC) for the city is listed on the same line.

The distance from the airport to the center city is given. Note the airport's three-letter city code is listed, in this example, SYD. Next car rental agencies at the airport are listed. Taxi information and prices to the center city are given. Airport bus and limo service operators are named if applicable. Their service is either S (scheduled) or NS (nonscheduled).

Airlines with service to the city are named and their phone numbers and ticket office locations are given. Some of these have toll-free numbers which are listed in a directory at the beginning of the book.

A key symbol indicates the beginning of the hotel/motel listings. First properties at or near the airport are given. Then downtown properties and those in other locations are listed.

As you can see from Figure 10-1, the first line of the hotel/motel listing is the property's name, address, and phone number. Room rates are given in a range. A dark square shows that at least an 8 percent commission is paid to travel agents. The letters *a, c, m,* indicate meal plans: American, Continental, and Modified American, respectively. A C and g indicate that corporate and government rates are available.

Referring again to Figure 10-1 note that the hotel/motel listings in the Pacific Asia edition include detailed information regarding facilities and services available at the property. This information is briefly included in the North American or European editions.

Figure 10-2 shows some representative listings from the European edition. Compare the listings shown in Figures 10-1 and 10-2 from the Pacific Asia and European editions, respectively, to the listing shown in Figure 10-3 from the North American edition for Las Vegas.

The hotel symbol indicates that the property is a member of the American Hotel and Motel Association. The *OAG Business Travel Planner* is the official lodging directory of the American Hotel and Motel Association. A rating system using one to five crowns is used in all the editions.

The *OAG Business Travel Planners* provide excellent city maps which show the proximity of some properties to the center city. Such a map is found for Las Vegas in the North American edition, as shown in Figure 10-4. Airport maps given in the *OAG Business Travel Planners*

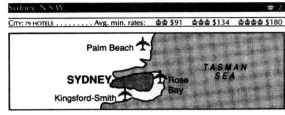

Sydney, N.S.W.

CITY: 79 HOTELS . . . . Avg. min. rates: 🏨🏨 $91 🏨🏨🏨 $134 🏨🏨🏨🏨 $180

SYDNEY AIRPORTS

✈ SYD (Kingsford Smith) 11.3 km/7 mi SW

AIRLINES

Aerolineas Argentinas (2 9283-3660) • Air Caledonie Intl (2 9321-9211) • Air China (2 9232-7277) • Air New Zealand (132476) • Air Pacific (1800-230150) • Air Vanuatu (2 9223-8333) • Air Zimbabwe • Alitalia (1300 653747) • All Nippon (2 9367-6711) • American (1800-620747) • Ansett (131767) • AOM French Arlns (2 9223-4444) • Asiana Arlns (133001) • British Airways (2 9258-3300) • Canadian Arlns Intl (2 9299-7843) • Cathay Pacific (131747) • China Eastern • Country Connection (6942-3500) • Egyptair (2 9232-6677) • EVA Airways (2 9221-7055) • Flight West • Garuda Indonesia (2 9334-9900) • Gulf Air (2 9321-9199) • Hazelton (131713) • Horizon Arlns (1800-810008) • Impulse Arlns (2 9317-4399) • Japan Airlines (2 9272-1111) • KLM (2 9231-6333) • Korean Air (2 9262-6000) • Lan Chile • Lauda Air (2 9367-3888) • Lufthansa • Malaysia Arlns (132627) • Mandarin Arlns (2 9321-9022) • National Jet (131313) • Olympic (1800 221663) • Polynesian Arlns (1300 653737) • Qantas (131313) • Royal Tongan Arlns (2 9244-2212) • Singapore Arlns (131011) • South African Airways (2 9223-4402) • Swissair (2 9232-1744) • Thai Arwys (2 9844-0999) • United (131777) • Vietnam Arlns (2 9252-3303) • Virgin Atlantic (1800-646747) • Yanda (131313)

AIRPORT CAR RENTALS

Kingsford Smith . . . . Avis • Budget • Dollar • Hertz • Thrifty

SYDNEY CLIMATE

		Jan	Feb	Mar	Apr	May	Jun	Jul	Aug	Sep	Oct	Nov	Dec
Average	(F)	65°	65°	63°	58°	52°	48°	46°	48°	51°	56°	60°	63°
Low	(C)	18°	18°	17°	14°	11°	9°	8°	9°	11°	13°	16°	17°
	(F)	78°	78°	76°	71°	66°	61°	60°	63°	67°	71°	74°	77°
High	(C)	26°	26°	24°	22°	19°	16°	16°	17°	19°	22°	23°	25°
	(in)	3.5	4.0	5.0	5.3	5.0	4.6	4.6	3.0	2.9	2.8	2.9	2.9
Rainfall	(mm)	89	102	127	135	127	117	117	76	74	71	74	74

SYDNEY TRANSPORTATION SUMMARY

DOWNTOWN TO AIRPORT: Schd. svc. . . . . .AUD 6-10 . . . . .20-40 min.

ATTRACTIONS

Australian Museum, 6 College St. 2 9320-6000
AMP Tower Centrepoint, Level 1 Centrepoint, Ste. 6 . . . . .2 9229-7444
Darling Harbour, ...
Koala Park Sanctuary, 84 Castle Hill Road (West Pennant Hills) 2 9484-3141
Macquarie Street, ...
Powerhouse Museum, 500 Harris St. (Ultimo) 2 9217-0111
Royal Botanic Gardens, Mrs. Macquaries Rd. 2 9231-8111
Sydney Aquarium, Aquarium Pier-Darling Harbour 2 9262-2300
Taronga Zoo, Bradleys Head Rd. (Mosman) 2 9969-2777
Wonderland Sydney, Wallgrove Rd. (Eastern Creek) 2 9830-9187

SYDNEY CONVENTION & EXHIBITION FACILITIES

MUNICIPAL FACILITIES

Sydney Conv & Exhibition Ctr • Darling Dr., Darling Harbour (Pyrmont) 2 9282-5000
Sydney Opera House • Bennelong Point 2 9250-7472
Sydney Showground & Exhib Complex • 1 Showground Rd. (Homebush Bay) 2 9704-1244

LOCAL INFORMATION

State Chamber of Commerce N.S.W. 2 9350-8100
Sydney Conv/Vis Bureau 2 9331-4045

CITY HOTELS

All Seasons Crown Hotel • 302/308 Crown St • (Darlinghurst 2010) • *Nr. Attr.* 2 9360-1133
NP $70-102 • *AUD* 110-160 • 🅲🅺 • RMS: 95 • CC:Most • RES: UI ■   FAX: 9380-8989
Amenities: Restaurant, Air Conditioning, TV, Kitchen Facilities, Refrigerator In-Room, Room Service, Non-Smoking Rooms, Handicapped Facilities.

All Seasons Premier Menzies Hotel • 14 Carrington St • 2001 • *In Downtown Area* 2 9299-1000
🏨🏨🏨 $190up • *AUD* 300 • 🅲 • RMS: 440 • MTG: 12 • CC:All ■   FAX: 9290-3819
RES: SSI, UI • Amenities: Restaurant, Meeting Rooms, Air Conditioning, Health Club, Bar, Conference Facilities, TV, Business Center.

ANA Hotel Sydney • 176 Cumberland St • 2000 • *In City Center* 2 9250-6000
🏨🏨🏨🏨 $216-314 • *AUD* 340-495 • 🅲 • RMS: 570 • MTG: 21 ■   FAX: 9250-6250
CC:All • RES: ANA, UI • Amenities: Restaurant, Meeting Rooms, Air Conditioning, Health Club, Bar, Conference Facilities, TV, Coffee Shop.

Astor Goldsbrough Apt Hotel • 243 Pyrmont St • 2009 • *In Business District* 2 9292-5000
RP 🅲 • RMS: 250 • CC:All ■   FAX: 9292-5699
Amenities: Restaurant, Air Conditioning, Health Club, TV, Coffee Shop, Business Center, Kitchen Facilities, Pool-Indoor.

Best Western City Beach Motor Inn • 99-103 Curlewis St • (Bondi Beach 2026) . . .2 9365-3100
🏨 $82-102 • *AUD* 130-160 • 🅲 • RMS: 25 • CC:All • RES: BW ■   FAX: 9365-0231
Amenities: Air Conditioning, Health Club, TV, Pool-Outdoor, Pool-Indoor, Refrigerator In-Room, Room Service, Handicapped Facilities.

FIGURE 10-1

Listings from the *OAG Travel Planner*, Pacific Asia Edition

show road access, gates, luggage retrieval, and shops and give approximate walking times from one end of the airport terminal to the other as well. See the representative airport map of Las Vegas McCarran International Airport shown in Figure 10-5.

Each edition gives the name, address, and phone numbers of hotel system representatives and reservation services. The two- and three-letter codes for these reps and systems are given in alphabetical order for cross-referencing.

All three editions give thorough information on passports, visas, and vaccination requirements for travel from the United States. How to obtain a passport and visa is indicated also.

Countries other than those in Europe and Asia Pacific are listed in the North American edition. Documentary requirements and consulate offices in the United States and Canada are given for these countries. The addresses and phone numbers for United States em-

Paris

PARIS
Charles De Gaulle
Orly

PARIS AIRPORTS
✈ **LBG** (Le Bourget) 12.9 km/8 mi N   ✈ **ORY** (Orly) 14.5 km/9 mi S
✈ **CDG** (Charles De Gaulle) 23.3 km/14.5 mi NE   ✈ **POX** (Paris Cergy Pontoise) 32.1 km/20 mi NW
✈ **BVA** (Tille) 72.4 km/45 mi NW

AIRLINES
Adria (1-47429500) • Aer Lingus (1-47421250) • Aeroflot (1-42254381) • Aeromexico (1-55-04-9010) • Air Afrique (1-44213333) • Air Algerie • Air Canada (1-44502020) • Air Charter • Air China (1-42661658) • Air Dolomiti (1-55604200) • Air Europa • Air France (0802-802802) • Air Gabon (1-43592063) • Air India (1-42684010) • Air Lanka (1-42974344) • Air Liberte (1-42790505) • Air Littoral (1-40677676) • Air Madagascar (1-43794210) • Air Malta (1-44860840) • Air Mauritius (1-44511564) • Air Moldova (1-42961010) • Air Normandie (1-47781414) • Air Seychelles (1-42898683) • Air Zimbabwe • Alitalia (1-44944400) • All Nippon (0800-908651) • American (1-69327307) • AOM French Arlns (0803-001234) • Armenian Airlines (1-42961010) • Austrian (0802-816816) • Avianca (1-42603522) • Balkan-Bulgarian (1-47426666) • Biman Bangladesh • British Airways (0802-802902) • British Midland (1-41918704) • Cameroon Arlns (1-43123010) • Cathay Pacific (1-41437500) • Chalair (2-33236363) • China Eastern • Continental (1-42990910) • Croatia Arlns (1-42653001) • Cronus Air • Crossair (0802-300400) • Cubana (1-45383112) • Cyprus Airways (1-45019338) • Czech Arlns (1-47423845) • Debonair • Delta (1-47689292) • Egyptair (1-44948520) • El Al (1-44550005) • Emirates (1-44959544) • Eurowings (1-48627938) • EVA Airways (1-41439111) • Finnair (1-47423333) • Gulf Air (1-49524141) • Hex'Air • Iberia (0802-075075) • Icelandair (1-44516051) • Iran Air (1-43590120) • Japan Airlines (1-44355500) • KLM (1-44561818) • KLM UK (1-44561800) • Korean Air (0800 6562001) • Kuwait Airways (1-47207515) • Lithuanian Arlns (1-53760875) • LOT (1-47420560) • Lufthansa (0802-020030) • Luxair (1-48625770) • Maersk Air (1-53771300) • Malaysia Arlns (1-44516420) • Malev (1-42660441) • Meridiana (1-42616150) • Middle East (1-42669393) • Northwest (1-42669000) • Olympic (1-42659242) • Pakistan Intl Arlns (1-45629241) • Qantas • Regional Arlns (1-49750448) • Royal Air Maroc (1-44931310) • Royal Jordanian (1-42444580) • Royal Nepal Arlns • Ryanair (3-44114141) • Sabena (0803-6678800) • SAS (0801-252525) • Saudi Arabian Arlns (1-53675050) • Singapore Arlns (1-45539090) • South African Airways (1-49270550) • Suckling Airways (1-48666894) • Swissair (0802-300-400) • Syrian Arab Arlns (1-47421197) • TAAG-Angola • TACV (1-56791313) • TAP Air Portugal (1-44836060) • Tarom (1-47422542) • Thai Arwys (1-44207080) • Tower Air (1-44515656) • Trans Aereos Meridionais • Tunis Air (1-42123131) • Turkish Airlines (1-42664740) • TWA (1-41919674) • Tyrolean Arwys (0802-300400) • Ukraine Intl Arlns (1-42930436) • Varig (0801-636162) • Vietnam Arlns (1-44543900) • Yemenia Yemen (1-42560600)

AIRPORT CAR RENTALS
Orly . . . . Auto Europe • Avis • Budget • Dollar (Europcar) • Europe by Car • Hertz • Kemwel (Citer) • Liddiard Travel • National • Payless • Thrifty
Charles De Gaulle . . Auto Europe • Avis • Budget • Dollar (Europcar) • Europe by Car • Hertz • Kemwel (Citer) • Liddiard Travel • National • Payless • Thrifty

PARIS CLIMATE

		Jan	Feb	Mar	Apr	May	Jun	Jul	Aug	Sep	Oct	Nov	Dec
Average	(F)	32°	33°	36°	41°	47°	52°	55°	55°	50°	44°	38°	33°
Low	(C)	0°	1°	2°	5°	8°	11°	13°	13°	10°	7°	3°	1°
High	(F)	42°	45°	52°	60°	67°	73°	76°	75°	69°	59°	49°	43°
	(C)	6°	7°	11°	16°	19°	23°	24°	24°	21°	15°	9°	6°
Rainfall	(in)	2.0	1.0	2.0	2.0	2.0	2.0	2.0	2.0	2.0	2.0	2.0	2.0
	(mm)	51	25	51	51	51	51	51	51	51	51	51	51

PARIS TRANSPORTATION SUMMARY
DOWNTOWN TO ORLY: Schd. svc. . . . . .FRF 35-70 . . . . .25-30 min.
DOWNTOWN TO CHARLES DE GAULLE:Schd. svc. . . . . .FRF 35-65 . . . . .30-50 min.
ORLY TO CHARLES DE GAULLE: Schd. svc. . . . . .FRF 70 . . . . .50 min.

LOCAL PUBLIC TRANSPORTATION
Public Transportation Information 1-43-46-14-14
Rail service between Charles de Gaulle Roissy Station & Gare du Nord or Chatelet; Travel Time 50 Min, Fare FRF 46.
Between Orly Airport & city center via Antony R.E.R. Station; Travel Time 6-30 Min, Fare FRF 52.
Shuttle service available from Austerlitz Station to Pont de Rungis; Travel Time 35 Min, Fare—FRF 28.00-42.50.
Rail service between Charles de Gaulle & Orly Airports; Travel Time 50 Min, Fare FRF 70.
Jetbus service to/from Villejuif-Louis Aragon Metro Station (Line 7);—Travel Time 30 Min, Fare FRF 22 (one way).

ATTRACTIONS
Arc de Triomphe, Place Charles de Gaulle 1-43-80-31-31
Bateaux Parisiens, Port de la Bourdonnais 1-44-11-33-44
Disneyland Paris, , (Marne-la-Vallee) 1-60-30-60-30
Eiffel Tower, Champ de Mars 1-45-50-34-56
Georges Pompidou Centre, Rue Beaubourg-Rue St. Martin 1-44-78-12-33
Lido de Paris, 116 Bis, Champs Elysees 1-40-76-56-10
Musee du Louvre, The Pyramid/Cow Napoleon .1-40-20-51-51
Museum of Science & Industry, 30 Ave. Corentin Cariou, Cedex 19 1-40-05-12-12
Notre Dame de Paris, Isle de'Cite 1-42-34-56-10
Orsay Museum, 1, Ue de la Legian d'Mahnewz .1-40-49-48-14

PARIS CONVENTION & EXHIBITION FACILITIES
MUNICIPAL FACILITIES
ALIOR • 6-10 rue du general Foy 1 44702320
Maison De La Chimie • 28, rue Saint-Dominique 1-40622700

Palais des Congres/Paris Conf. Centre • 2 Place de la Porte Maillot 1-40682550

LOCAL INFORMATION
Central Post Office 1-40-28-20-38/0801 630201
City Hall of Paris- Information Office 1-42-76-43-43
Lost & Found Bureau 1-55-76-20-20
Office of Tourism 1-49-52-53-95
Paris Chamber of Commerce & Industry 1-55-65-55-65
Paris Convention & Visitors Bureau 1-49-52-53-95

CITY HOTELS
Aberotel Montparnasse • 24 rue Blomet • *In City Center* 1-40-61-70-50
$54-107 • *FRF* 330-650 • ⬛⬛ • RMS: 28 • CC:Most ■   FAX: 1-40-61-08-31
RES: UI
Abotel Acropole • 199 blvd Brune • 75014 • *In City Center* 1-45-39-64-17
$77-126 C • *FRF* 470-772 • ⬛⬛ • RMS: 43 • CC:Most ■   FAX: 1-47-27-05-87
RES: ABO, MIN
Abotel Alma Elysees • 32 rue de l'Exposition • 75007 • *In Downtown Area* 1-47-05-45-70
$77-118 C • *FRF* 470-722 • RMS: 32 • MTG: 1 • CC:All ■   FAX: 1-47-27-05-87
RES: ABO, STI

FIGURE 10-2

Listings from the *OAG Travel Planner,* European Edition

bassies abroad are listed. Climate, how to phone, taxes, time zone, customs allowances, and information addresses also are given.

The European and Pacific Asia editions are distinguished from the North American by being alphabetized by country then city. Country listings in these two editions give information regarding documentary requirements, consulate addresses, chambers of commerce addresses, climate, communications, currency, electric current, taxes/tipping, and information addresses. Government hotel ratings are defined.

Las Vegas, NV (cont'd from p. 366)
CITY HOTELS

A Algiers Hotel • 2845 Las Vegas Blvd S • 89109 • *In City Center* 702 735-3311
   ȼȼ $35-125 • Ⓒ • RMS: 105 • RES: ERS ■   FAX: 792-2112

Ambassador East Motel • 916 E Fremont St • 89101 • *In Downtown Area* 702 384-8281
   RMS: 102 • MTG: 1 • Rest. ■

A AmeriSuites • 4520 Paradise Rd • 89109 . . . . .702 369-3366
   NP $59-109 c • ⒸⒺ • RMS: 279 • MTG: 9 • Rest. • RES: ASH, LRB ■   FAX: 369-0009

A Arizona Charlie's • 740 S Decatur Ave • 89107 • *Near Airport* 702 258-5200
   $48-69 • ⒸⒺ • RMS: 253 • Exec. flr. • Rest. ■   FAX: 258-5192

Bally's Las Vegas - Hilton Casino • 3645 Las Vegas Blvd S • 89109 . . . . .702 739-4111
   ȼȼȼ $99up • RMS: 2814 • MTG: 52 • Exec. flr. • Rest. • RES: HRW ■   FAX: 967-3848

A Barbary Coast • 3595 Las Vegas Blvd S • 89109 • *In Suburban Area* 702 737-7111
   ȼȼȼ $49-159 • ⒸⒺ • RMS: 200 • Rest. • Rm. Svc. • RES: LHS ■   FAX: 737-6304

A Barcelona Hotel • 5011 E Craig Rd • 89115 • *Near Tourist Area* 702 644-6300
   $35up • RMS: 177 • Rm. Svc.   FAX: 644-6510

Bellagio Hotel • 3600 Las Vegas Blvd So • 89109 • *At Attractions* 702 693-7111
   NP $150-500 • RMS: 3005 • MTG: 58 • Exec. flr. • Rest. • RES: SCE ■   FAX: 693-8777

A Best Western Heritage Inn • 4975 S Valley View • *Near Airport* 702 798-7736
   ȼȼȼ $69-105 c • Ⓔ • RMS: 65 • MTG: 50 • RES: BW ■

A Best Western Main Street Inn • 1000 N Main St • 89101 • *Nr. Cty. Ctr.* 702 382-3455
   ȼȼ $50-135 c • Ⓒ • RMS: 91 • Rest. • RES: BW ■   FAX: 382-1428

Best Western Nellis Motor Inn • 5330 E Craig Rd • 89115 • *In Subr. Area* 702 643-6111
   ȼȼ $65up • Ⓒ • RMS: 52 • RES: BW ■   FAX: 643-8553

Best Western Parkview Inn • 921 Las Vegas Blvd N • 89101 • *In Dwtn. Area* 702 385-1213
   ȼ ⒸⒺ • RMS: 56 • RES: BW ■

A Binions Horseshoe Hotel & Casino • 128 E Fremont St • 89101 . . . . .702 382-1600
   ȼȼ $35-65 • RMS: 379 • Rest. • Rm. Svc. ■   FAX: 384-1574

Blair House Suites • 344 E Desert Inn Rd • 89109 • *Near Attractions* 702 792-2222
   ȼȼ $125up • Ⓒ • STE: 224 • MTG: 2 • RES: ERS ■   FAX: 792-9042

Boulder Manor • 4823 Boulder Hwy • 89121 . . . . .702 456-2104
   $149-169   FAX: 456-2139

A Boulder Station Hotel & Casino • 4111 Boulder Hwy • 89121 • *On Hwy.* 702 432-7777
   ȼȼȼ $49-119 • RMS: 300 • MTG: 4 • Rest. • Rm. Svc. ■   FAX: 432-7708

A Bourbon Street Hotel • 120 E Flamingo Rd • 89109 • *In Resort Area* 702 737-7200
   ȼ $65up • ⒸⒺ • RMS: 196 • MTG: 2 • Rest. • Rm. Svc. • RES: LRB, NRB ■   FAX: 734-9155

A Budget Inn • 301 S Main St • 89101 • *In Tourist Area* 702 385-5560
   RP $33-105 • ⒸⒺ • RMS: 81 ■   FAX: 382-9273

A Caesars Palace • 3570 Las Vegas Blvd S • 89109 • *In Resort Area* 702 731-7110
   ȼȼȼȼ $169up • RMS: 2400 • MTG: 34 • Exec. flr. • Rest. • RES: LRB ■   FAX: 731-7172

California Hotel Casino & RV Park • 12 E Ogden Ave • 89101 . . . . .702 385-1222
   ȼȼ $40-80 • RMS: 781 • MTG: 2 • Exec. flr. • Rest. • Rm. Svc. ■   FAX: 388-2660

The Carriage House • 105 E Harmon Ave • 89109 • *In Resort Area* 702 798-1020
   ȼȼȼ $89-135 • Ⓒ • STE: 155 • MTG: 1 • Rest. • Rm. Svc. ■   FAX: 798-1020

A Casino Royale Hotel • 3411 Las Vegas Blvd South • 89109 • *In Rsrt. Area* 702 737-3500
   ȼȼ Rest. • Rm. Svc.   FAX: 650-4743

Center Strip Inn • 3688 Las Vegas Blvd S • 89109 • *In Resort Area* 702 739-6066
   ȼ Ⓒ • RMS: 156 • RES: ERS ■   FAX: 736-2521

Circus Circus Hotel & Casino • 2880 Las Vegas Blvd S • 89109 . . . . .702 734-0410
   ȼȼȼ $19-220 • RMS: 2787 • Rest. • Rm. Svc. • RES: LHS, LRB ■   FAX: 734-5897

A Club Hotel by Doubletree-Las Vegas Airpo • 7250 Pollock Dr • 89119 . . . . . . .702 948-4000
   NP $89-99 • ⒸⒺ • RMS: 190 • MTG: 3 • Rest. • RES: DBT ■   FAX: 948-4100

Convention Center Lodge • 79 E Convention Center Dr • 89109 . . . . .702 735-1315
   RMS: 56   FAX: 735-1807

Courtyard by Marriott • 3275 Paradise Rd • 89109 • *In Resort Area* 702 791-3600
   ȼȼȼ $79-229 • Ⓒ • RMS: 149 • MTG: 1 • Rest. • Rm. Svc. • RES: CBM ■   FAX: 796-7981

Crest Motel • 207 N 6th St • 89101 • *In Downtown Area* 702 382-5642
   $25-50 c • RMS: 154 • RES: ERS ■   FAX: 382-8038

Days Inn Airport • 5125 Swenson • 89119 • *Near Attractions* 702 740-4040
   ȼȼ $45-85 • Ⓒ • RMS: 327 • MTG: 1 • Rest. • Rm. Svc. • RES: DAY ■   FAX: 795-2325

Days Inn Downtown • 707 E Fremont St • 89101 • *In Downtown Area* 702 388-1400
   ȼȼ $28-119 • ⒸⒺ • RMS: 147 • Rest. • Rm. Svc. • RES: DAY ■   FAX: 388-9622

A Days Inn Town Hall Casino • 4155 Koval Lane • 89109 • *In Resort Area* 702 731-2111
   ȼ $35-200 • ⒸⒺ • RMS: 357 • Rest. • RES: DAY ■   FAX: 731-1113

Debbie Reynolds Hotel & Casino • 305 Convention Center Dr • 89109 . . . . .702 734-0711
   ȼȼ $59-75 • ⒸⒺ • RMS: 193 • MTG: 2 • Rest. • Rm. Svc. ■   FAX: 734-7548

FIGURE 10-3

Listings from the *OAG Travel Planner,* North American Edition

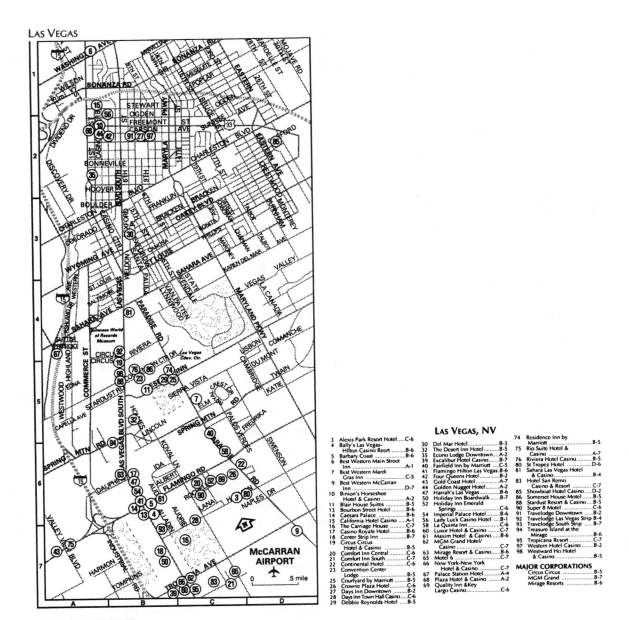

FIGURE 10-4

Map of Las Vegas, Nevada, with hotel key from the North American Edition of the *OAG Travel Planner*

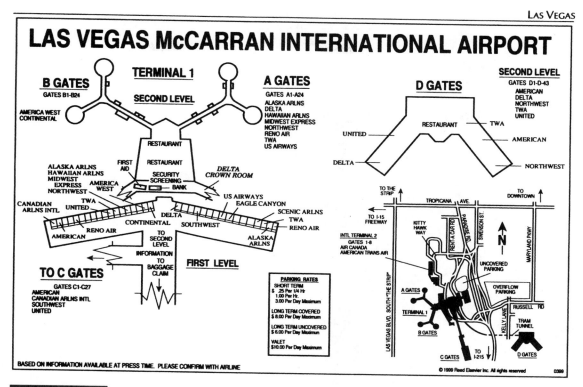

FIGURE 10-5

Map of the Las Vegas McCarran International Airport from the *OAG Travel Planner,* North American Edition

All in all, the *OAG Business Travel Planners* are excellent hotel/motel reference books which provide a wealth of information on both domestic and international travel. They serve the travel industry well.

THE INTERNET

The Internet links computers throughout the world. The World Wide Web enables travelers to book their own hotel room directly. If you are not familiar with using the Internet and subsequently its Web pages, some patience is in order. As someone said, "The Internet is like having an encyclopedia at your fingertips, but it is not alphabetized."

If you know the name and approximate address of a property and wish to make a reservation, the Yellow Pages may give you a Web address and/or telephone number. If you know that you prefer a certain

brand or chain, that name can be typed in the *Search* slot to view its Web site. Then scroll through and choose the desired location, by country, state, and city. Descriptions, and often a map, of each of the chain's properties in a city are shown. City convention and visitor bureaus usually have Web sites, and many include hotel lists and reservation information. Keying the city name in the *Search* slot should give the CVB's Web site as a selection.

If "hotel" is typed into the *Search* slot, a list of chains and brands is shown. Scroll through and click on your choice. Then scroll through and click on your desired location. The Web site that appears will often show pictures of the specific property and give detailed information on amenities and price range.

Major travel sites on the Web are Travelocity, Preview Travel, Expedia, and Internet Travel Network. Once in them, click on the "accommodations" option. Destination selections will be followed by chain and brand options. Additional sites are www.all-hotels.com, www.hotelguide.com, www.frommers.com, www.fodors.com.

Reservations may be made directly through the Internet. In order to do this you must know the specific dates that you require reservations and be prepared to give your credit card number and expiration date. Most sites have disclaimers stating that credit card information is encrypted to protect the purchases.

Following are step-by-step operations for making reservations at a specific property.

To enter the site, click *Internet* then click *Go to Web*. At *Search* blank, type in "hotels."

SCREEN	CLICK
Several options show current travel bargains	*Hotel directory*
Advertising	*Hotel index*
Lists chains	Make choice (ex: Marriott Hotels)
Shows Marriott Web page	*Hotel directory*
List of brands	Make choice (ex: Marriott Hotels, Resorts and Suites)
Asks where, by country and state	Scroll to desired (ex: District Columbia)
Lists properties	Click desired (ex: Marriott Pa. Ave.)

Picture of hotel and description including number of rooms, restaurants, amenities	Click *Make reservation*
Blanks for *Date of arrival* and *Date of departure*	Scroll to fill in
Number of adults	Scroll to fill in
Blanks for identification numbers (i.e., travel agent)	Fill in
	Click *Availability*
Select rate followed by description such as city view, kind of bed, concierge, AARP, government	Click choice
Name, address, phone, credit card blanks	Fill in
	Hit *Send form*

Warnings may be posted to click *Send form* only once to avoid double booking.

For international properties such as Intercontinental Hotels, first the continent (sometimes shown by a map), then region, then country/city are asked for. Prices may be shown in the country's currency.

TRENDS

Use of the Internet to make and guarantee hotel reservations is one of the biggest changes in the accommodation industry. As individuals access information on, and make reservations with, specific hotels, computer knowledge becomes more vital for front-desk and reservation personnel. Travel agents who are expert in accessing the Internet to obtain availability on specific dates and rate information will be in demand. In spite of detailed information on meeting capacities, meeting planners will still visit properties to assess their usefulness before booking rooms for a conference. The leisure traveler who is seriously shopping for low-priced accommodations will still telephone direct to the hotel in hopes of a yield management situation where individual properties can quote lower than what is published on the Internet or central reservation system.

CHAPTER ACTIVITIES

ACCOMMODATIONS: REFERENCES AND RATINGS

1. Name three hotel/motel information sources.

2. List three advantages and disadvantages for the sources you listed.

3. Name six pieces of information that the *OAG Travel Planners* give on each country.

CHAPTER PROJECTS

1. Visit a local travel agency and see which hotel/motel reference sources they use.

2. Describe the Internet screens you see and operations you perform to make a reservation at the
   a. Mark Hopkins Hotel in San Francisco
   b. Intercontinental Ritz in Lisbon, Portugal

GLOSSARY

A

AAA   American Automobile Association.

AARP   American Association of Retired People.

adjacent or adjoining rooms   Rooms located side by side that do not necessarily have a connecting door.

all-inclusive   Travel arrangements where all costs are covered in one prepaid price, i.e., transportation, accommodations, meals, and often beverages, tax, and tips.

American Plan   All meals are included in the cost of the room.

associations   An organization of people who have a common interest, be it personal or professional.

B

bank   The amount of money given a cashier at the beginning of the shift. The bank must be reconciled at the end of that shift with cash payments, checks cashed, and paid outs.

bed and breakfasts (B & Bs)   Lodging facilities which include breakfast in the cost of the room. The term is used primarily in the United Kingdom.

blocked rooms   A number of rooms reserved at the same time, usually for a convention or tour group.

boatels   Accommodations on boats.

branding   A hospitality company that gives different names to different types of hotels that serve a certain type of clientele. A large chain may have several "brands" with different names and marketing strategies.

bucket   Usually a metal, oblong box on rollers that contains guests' folios.

bus people   Restaurant employees who clean and reset the tables. They assist the waiters and waitresses.

C

caravansary   An inn or hotel where caravans stopped overnight, primarily in the Middle East and Orient. Usually buildings surround a courtyard.

catering/banquet department   The hotel department that plans and sometimes serves and prepares meals for groups at the hotel.

chain   A group of affiliated hotel/motels that usually carry the same name and share established operating policies, common reservation systems, and decor standards.

checker   The employee who inspects a room after room cleaners have cleaned it.

chief engineer   The head of the engineering department in a hotel.

city ledger   The account that shows all money owed to the hotel except that owed by guests currently staying there. Credit card charges, personal charges, and overlooked charges are reflected in it.

concierge service (pronounced: con-c-erzh)   Personalized service to VIP guests. The term *concierge* is the title given to the person in charge of providing these special services.

condo (condominium)   An apartment house where individual apartments are owned by private individuals who pay fees for the upkeep of the common areas. Often these are rented as vacation accommodations.

conference and visitor bureaus (CVBs)   Organizations within a city or county with membership made up of tourism-related businesses. Joint advertising and promotions are carried out to increase visitors to the area.

connecting rooms   Rooms located side by side with a door between them.

continental plan   Breakfast is included in the cost of the room.

controller   The employee in charge of the fiscal matters at a hotel/motel.

convention services manager (CSM)   The person in a property who is assigned to a group that is holding an event within the premises. He serves as primary contact between the group and other hotel staff.

D

day rate   The rate charged in a property for use of a room only during the day.

discrepancy report   The difference between the rooms listed as ready for rental according to the front desk and those listed ready according to the Housekeeping department.

DNA (did not arrive)   A guest who had a reservation but did not check in to the hotel.

DNS (did not stay)   A guest who checked in to a hotel but did not stay there.

double-double room   A room that can accommodate two to four people with two double or queen-size beds.

double room   A room that can accommodate two people in a double or queen-size bed.

due-outs   Guests who are expected to check out.

E

EAP　Each additional person. The extra charge made when additional persons in a room exceed its capacity designation, such as double or triple.

Elderhostel　An organization that sponsors package tours for senior citizens. These often include educational activities.

engineering department　The department that handles the maintenance and repair of the physical plant, i.e., electricity, plumbing, renovating.

en suite　The term used to describe rooms with private baths. The term is used most often in Europe describing bed and breakfasts.

European plan (EAP)　No meals are included in the cost of the room.

executive chef　The manager of all food preparation.

executive housekeeper　The employee in charge of the cleaning staff.

F

FIFO　First in–first out. Used in inventory control to promote the utilization of items that have been "on the shelf" the longest time.

floor limit　The amount of credit available to a guest as specified by the credit card company.

folio　A running tabulation of the charges a guest has incurred from all the departments of the hotel.

food and beverage manager　The employee who supervises all staff dealing with food and beverage preparation, serving, and purchasing.

forecasts　The reports that estimate the number of guests to occupy the hotel at a particular period.

franchise　Property that is a part of a national or regional chain or management company sharing the name, a central reservation network, and advertising. The property is not owned by the chain or management company but pays a fee for the shared benefits.

frequent-user programs　Programs that reward travelers that are loyal to one particular brand of airline, hotel, or rental car business.

front office　The nerve center of the hotel that typically includes the front desk, uniformed services, the switchboard, and reservations.

full-service　Properties that provide a range of services, usually including a restaurant on the premises, luggage assistance, and room service.

G

general manager (GM)   The chief executive officer of a hotel, ultimately responsible for all its activities.

group sales   Sales of more than an individual room. These might be for group meetings or for tour groups.

guaranteed reservation   A reservation for which the first night has been paid in advance. The room will be held until checkout time the following day.

guest houses   Private homes with bedrooms for rent. Often a bath is shared with other guests or with the family.

H

hostel   Origin of the term "hotel" which denotes an inn or lodging place. In today's usage, the term indicates lesser quality or group dormitorylike accommodations.

hosteler   Historically, the term referred to the owner of a lodging establishment or person who worked at a lodging establishment. Today's meaning is a person who stays at a hostel.

hotel   Multistoried lodging facilities, usually located in city environments which range in size from 20 rooms to hundreds of rooms.

hotel representative   A person or company that handles reservations and group sales for independent properties. A 1-800 reservation number might be used.

housekeeping department   The department in charge of cleaning both guest rooms and public areas. It might also manage maintenance and renovation.

house staff   The workers who set up meeting and dining rooms for groups.

I

incentive travel   Awards or prizes of free travel given to top business performers, usually for excellence in sales.

Intourist   The national tourism organization of Russia.

K

kitchen steward   The person in charge of nonfood activities in a restaurant kitchen, including cleanup, sanitation, and linen and china supplies.

L

limited-service   Properties that provide primarily sleeping rooms without other amenities such as food service.

long room   Historically, the sleeping room of an inn. All guests slept in one room with their feet toward the fireplace.

M

maitre d'   The person in charge of serving the guests in the dining room. The maitre d' oversees hosting, table service, and bus personnel.

media   Communications channels for advertising such as newspapers, magazines, broadcasting, billboards, and the internet.

meeting planner   The person who organizes conventions, conferences, board meetings, seminars, trade shows, social events, or any gathering for an organization or business group.

modified American plan   Two meals are included in the price of the room, which are breakfast plus lunch or dinner.

motel   Lodging facilities usually found on feeder highways and roads, with parking in front of or near the room. Motels are most often one-story structures.

motor inns   Lodging facilities usually located near major highways wherein guests park their own cars in the vicinity of their rooms. Motor inns range in height from two to six stories.

N

night auditor   The person who finalizes the hotel's accounts for each day, updating credits and debits for each room rental and for each hotel department. Summaries for the day's business and forecasts for the future are made.

nonrevenue (nonrev)   No payment is received by the property. Usually used in reference to people, such as meeting planners or VIPs, who are not charged for accommodations.

no-show   A person with a reservation who does not come to the hotel.

O

OC (on change)   A room that has been vacated by a guest and is scheduled to be cleaned by the housekeeping department.

occupancy rate   The available rooms divided by the number of rooms actually occupied.

OOO (out of order)   A room that cannot be occupied because of a cosmetic or mechanical problem.

ordinary   Historic term used, particularly in Britain, for taverns or lodging establishments.

outside contractor   A person who does not work for the hotel, but who is hired to complete a specific maintenance or construction job.

overstays (stay-overs)   Guests who remain at the hotel longer than the length of their original reservation.

P

package plan   A trip for which a person pays one price which includes two or more components of tourism, such as transportation and accommodations.

paid outs   Money that is paid by the cashier for incidentals such as COD deliveries, or to reimburse a bellhop for a tip that was charged to a guest's folio.

paradores   Government-owned properties in Spain. Often these are renovated historic buildings and charge reasonable rates.

pensiones   Term used primarily in Europe to denote a guest house.

PIA (paid in advance)   A prepayment for a room which is included with the reservation.

POS (point of sale)   The place where a sale is made. This might be the front desk, restaurant, or gift shop. A POS computer can automatically enter the charge in the guest folio the moment the transaction occurs.

post roads   The roads used by the United States Postal Service when it was established in the early eighteenth century.

pousadas   Government-owned properties in Portugal. Often these are renovated historic buildings and charge reasonable rates.

profile   Data that show the preferences of regular clients or guests of a hotel. Demographics of the guest and characteristics, such as type of room and use of business facilities, are recorded for future reference.

Property Management Systems (PMS)   Computer programs that perform much of the tedious night auditor's accounting duties.

public areas   Areas in a hotel/motel that are not private rooms but are used by guests of the hotel. These include the lobby, public rest rooms, and meeting rooms.

purchasing steward   The employee in the food and beverage department who purchases all food products.

Q

quad   A room that can accommodate four people in double or twin beds.

R

rack rate (room rate)   The standard rate a sleeping room is assigned.

ready rooms   Rooms that have been cleaned and are ready for the occupancy of the next guest.

rebate voucher   The form given a guest that indicates a credit is due the folio. This might be for an overcharge on a meal or an incorrect phone charge.

receiving steward The employee in the food and beverage department who inspects, properly stores, and inventories all food coming into the restaurant.

registration card The card an incoming guest completes at the front desk during the registration process. It acts as a contract between the guest and the hotel.

regular reservation A reservation that has not been paid for in advance. If the guest does not arrive by a specified time, the reservation will be released and the room sold to a walk-in.

residential clients Those guests who live at a hotel/motel on a weekly, monthly, or annual basis. They are usually given a less-expensive rate.

resorts Hotel/motels usually located at popular vacation locations which offer recreational activities such as golf, tennis, or casino gambling.

RFP (Request for Proposals) Documents sent to vendors that give the specifications for a product or activity and that invite the company to offer a bid for such.

RNA (registered but not assigned) A person who has registered with the hotel but has not yet been assigned a room. This might occur if there is not yet a cleaned room ready for occupancy.

ROH (Run-of-the-House) No specific location within the property is designated for the reservation. The property chooses the room to offer to the guest. No special requests, such as beach front or third floor are honored.

room board A board, usually located behind the front desk, with slots for each room indicating that room's status. A registration card inserted in a slot would indicate the room is occupied. Colored plastic over the room's slot might indicate that the room is being cleaned.

room cleaners The workers who physically clean the guest rooms.

rooming slip A form or copy or portion of the registration card that is given to the guest. It indicates the guest's name, room number, and room rate.

room rack See ***room board.***

room rate See ***rack rate.***

S

sales department The department responsible for finding occupants for each room, each night, at the highest rate possible. It is also the department responsible for filling meeting rooms.

service Conduct that is useful or helpful to others.

single room   A room that can accommodate one person with a twin or double bed.

skippers   People who depart the property without paying their bills.

sleepers   A room that does not show on the room rack or computer as being available for occupancy, although it is available. This results in lost revenue for the hotel.

slept-outs   Guests who have paid for a room but did not sleep there.

smart card   A card that can be programmed to hold great quantities of information, such as identification, nationality, credit, and health. These can be programmed to open locks.

spas   Pools or springs thought to be of medicinal value and around which beautiful resorts were often built.

stay-overs   See *overstays.*

suite   A guest space which contains a living room and one or more bedrooms.

switchboard   The central telephone mechanism. Incoming and outgoing calls process through it.

T

table d'hote   "Table of the house or hotel." A meal is selected from a limited menu.

time and charges   A request made of the long distance operator in order that a call can be properly billed.

time-sharing   A specific period of rental time that is bought at a hotel or condominium.

time stamp   A clock that can imprint the date and time on various paperwork, or incoming mail, and messages.

tourist courts   A term used to denote a small motel. These were usually roadside lodging establishments with parking in front of the individual rooms.

tour operators   People or companies that put together the components of a tour or package vacation. They deal with the transportation, hotel/motel, and sightseeing facets of tourism from a wholesaler's perspective.

tower concept   Rooms, usually on the top floor of a property, that are set aside for VIPs. Usually concierge service is offered. A key in the elevator allows access only to those residing there.

trade shows   An exhibit of merchandise for sale usually concerning one field of business. These are held in conjunction with meetings and conventions.

transfers   Travel arrangements that move people from one place to another, usually from their primary transportation (for example, from the airport) to their place of accommodation.

transient clients Vacation or business travelers who stay at a lodging facility for a short time, not on a regular basis.

triple room A room that can accommodate three people either in a double and a single bed, three twin beds, or two double beds.

twin-double room A room that can accommodate two people with two twin beds.

U

understays Guests who do not stay at the hotel for the entire time they initially indicated.

V

voucher A form that indicates that a charge has been made by a guest. For example, a guest charges lunch and the restaurant draws up a voucher which is sent to the front desk to be included in the guest's folio.

W

walk-in A person with no reservation who appears at the property desiring a room.

walk-outs See ***skippers.***

walk the guest A hotel places a guest in another hotel. This occurs when a guest has a reservation which, for some reason, the hotel cannot honor.

wine steward The person in charge of alcoholic beverage service. The wine steward might also be in charge of purchasing and taking inventory of beverages.

Y

yield management A financial management method of pricing and capacity control that yields maximum profits. History, occupancy data, and competition are among the considerations used in this method.

INDEX

HOTEL/MOTEL OPERATIONS
AN OVERVIEW

2ND EDITION